Discursive Dress

John Michael Kohler Arts Center
Sheboygan, Wisconsin

Published on the occasion of an exhibition organized and presented by the John Michael Kohler Arts Center, Sheboygan, Wisconsin, September 26, 1993 - January 2, 1994. Supported in parts by grants from the National Endowment for the Arts and the Wisconsin Arts Board.

Printed in the United States of America.

Library of Congress Cataloging-in-Publication Data

Discursive Dress
p. cm.
Includes bibliographical references and index.
"Published on the occasion of an exhibition organized and presented by the John Michael Kohler Arts Center, Sheboygan, Wisconsin, September 26, 1993 - January 2, 1994."
ISBN 0-932718-37-X
1. Clothing and dress in art—Exhibitions.
2. Art, Modern—20th century—Exhibitions.
I. John Michael Kohler Arts Center.
N8217.C63D57
709'.73'07477569—dc20
94-30560
CIP

Front Cover: Christine LoFaso, *Redress: Gestation Corset and Codpiece*, detail

Back Cover: *Redress: Gestation Corset and Codpiece*, detail, 1992, 23½ x 16 x 13" corset only

Table of Contents

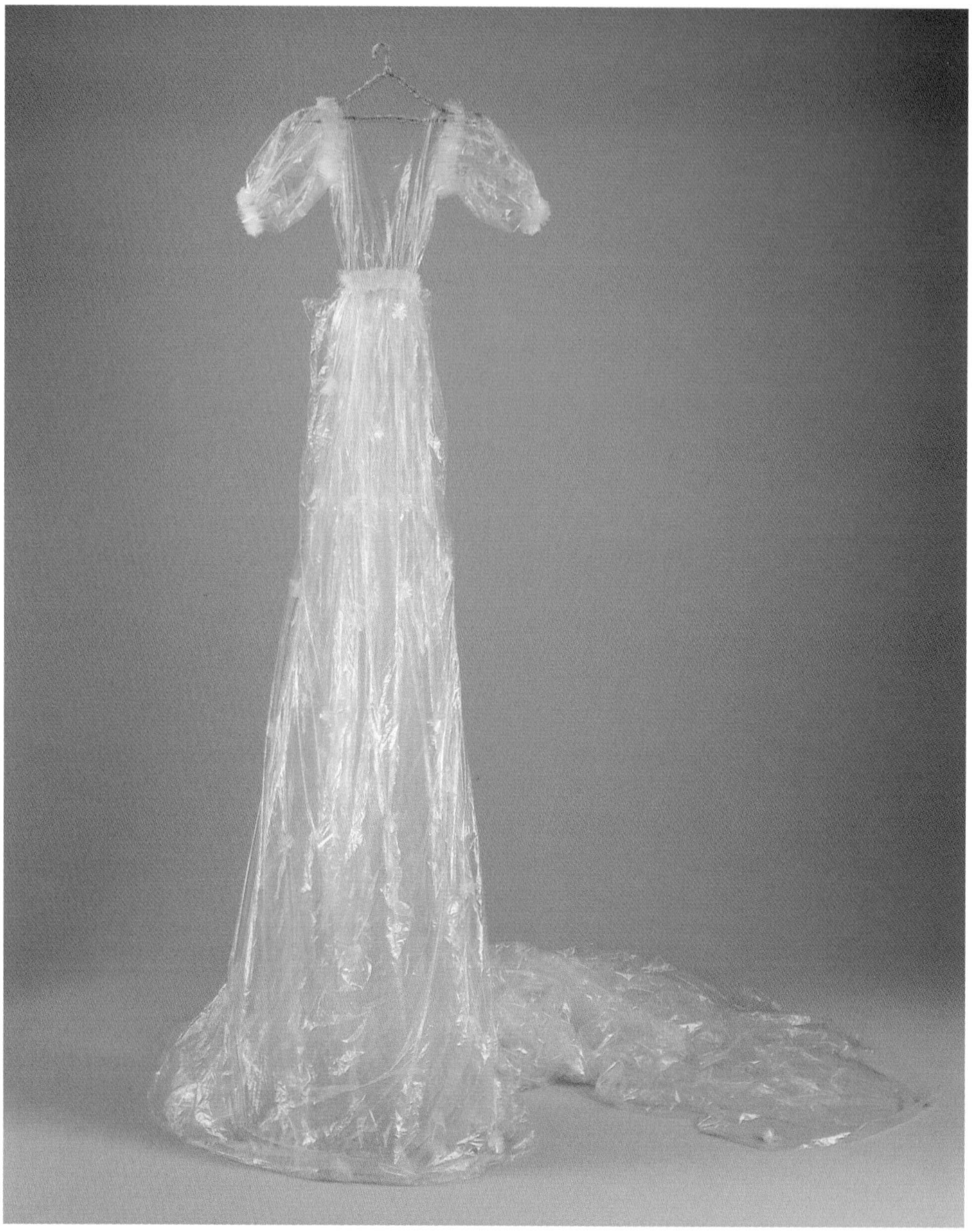

Elizabeth Leister, *Untitled (Wedding Dress)*, 1992, 124 x 58 x 97"

Acknowledgements

Discursive Dress is the second of three exhibitions and related publications which combine an exploration of material with that of social and cultural issues. Developed by John Michael Kohler Arts Center Curator of Exhibitions Alison Ferris, the series presents compelling bodies of work in contexts designed to stimulate viewers and readers to analyze and question conventional thinking about material-based work. The first in the series, Hair (1992), included work by 26 artists who use hair as a stand-in for the human body: to symbolize and investigate issues of mortality, fetishism, and "difference" and to challenge formal aspects of image making. The third in the series (1995) will focus on "conceptual textiles" by artists whose work is textile based and joins craft with issues such as domesticity, the body, masculinity, femininity, ethnicity, child abuse, and power. By showing that content and form can coexist, these artists challenge the authoritative precedents of contemporary art as well as simplified, incomplete understandings of textiles and their history.

The artists in Discursive Dress use clothing to offer their perspectives on various aspects of our society. As with all exhibitions at the John Michael Kohler Arts Center, Discursive Dress has involved multiple components that have aided in elucidating the work of these artists: this publication and a variety of other interpretive materials; video interviews with several artists; a residency with Christine LoFaso during which she worked with hundreds of high school, undergraduate, and graduate students in lecture-discussions and the creation of clothing-based work; and other educational programming, from participatory tours to gallery talks and classes.

This undertaking has been made possible only through the joint efforts of many individuals and organizations. The John Michael Kohler Arts Center expresses its profound thanks to the 175 corporations and foundations and over 1,350 families who provide the ongoing support of the program and operations. Our gratitude is also extended to the National Endowment for the Arts and the Wisconsin Arts Board for their understanding of the significance of the project and their financial commitment to it.

Our deep appreciation goes out to the participating artists, for they and their work are the heart of Discursive Dress. We also acknowledge the generosity of the following individuals and organizations that have lent works or otherwise have been of particular assistance: Susan Canning, John D'Anieri, Allan Dinsfriend, Ronald Feldman Fine Arts, Inc., Barbara Krakow Gallery, Galerie Lallouz & Watterson, R. Anne McCarthy, Robert Raczka, Stux Gallery, Germans van Eck Gallery, and Elga Wimmer Gallery.

We are grateful to our steadfast docents and other Friends of Art volunteers, our Artists Advisory Board, and the Board of Directors of the Sheboygan Arts Foundation, Inc. for their constant support of our endeavors. Finally, we express our boundless praise to the Arts Center staff for their dedication, their skill, and unflagging teamwork.

Ruth DeYoung Kohler

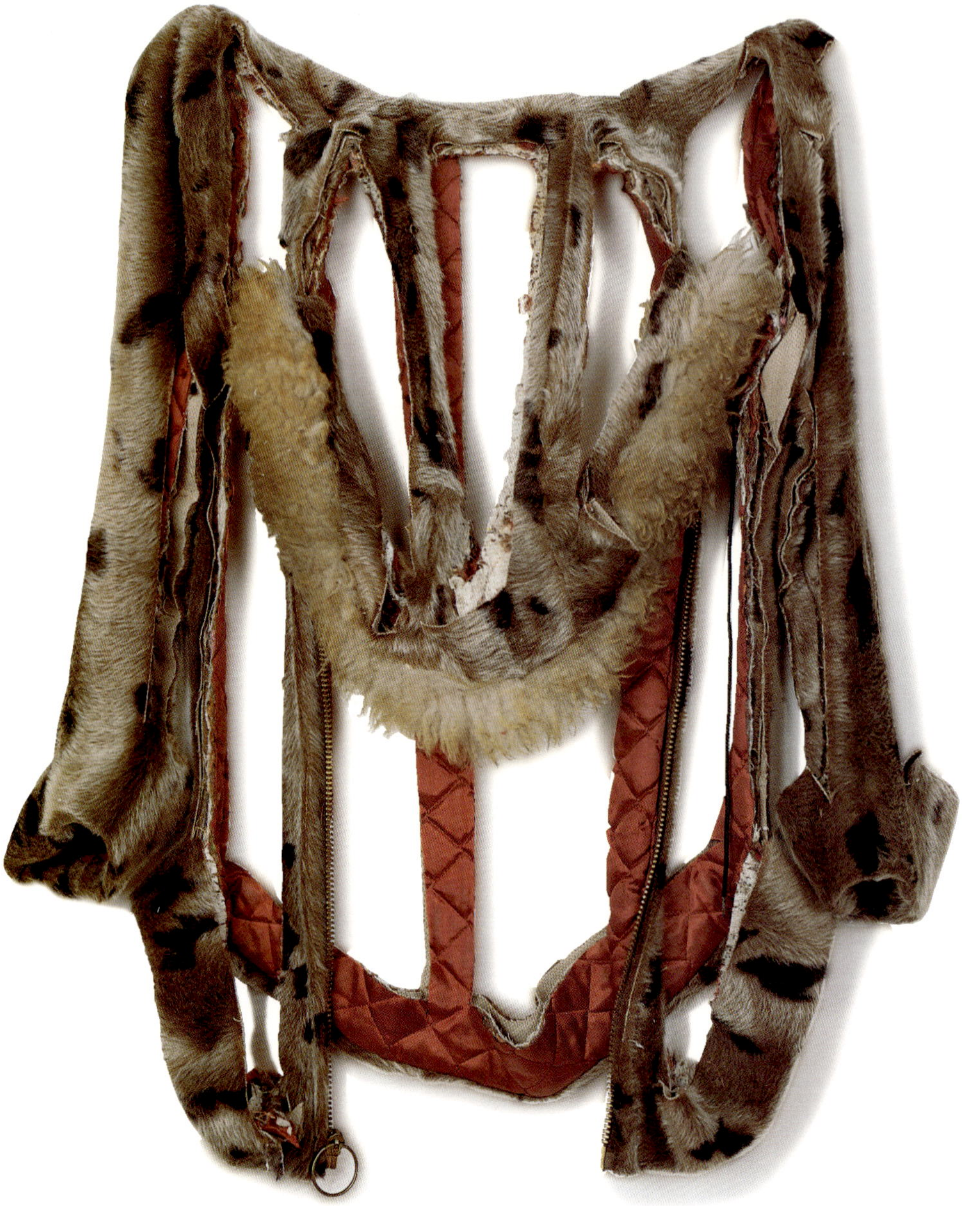

Jesse Goode, *Coats*, detail, 1991, 164½ x 230½ x 5¼"

Discursive Dress

"Dress is always unspeakably meaningful."
—Elizabeth Wilson, *Adorned in Dreams*

The "Meaning" of Clothing

Jesse Goode's *Coats* (cat. no. 7, illus. p. viii), altered beyond function and lining the wall like skeletons, serves as a metaphor for how to look at clothing in order to understand its meaning. Goode displays only the structures of the coats, that is, the seams of the garment with the bulk of the material cut out. Usually taken for granted, structures frame forms but are less noticeable or invisible in the final product. In *Coats*, our expectations of clothing's cohesion, both physical and symbolic, are made evident by Goode's "destruction" of them. Similarly, an examination of the discourses that structure the meanings of clothes can reveal interpretations other than those gleaned from the surface.

The title, *Discursive Dress*, was inspired by the notion of "discursive formation," a term used by the French philosopher Michel Foucault to address the systematic interconnections between an assortment of related statements which define a field of knowledge. Today, the meaning of clothing evolves from overlapping and changing discourses of class, race, popular culture, high fashion, feminism, academia, subcultures, anthropology, the entertainment industry, and the history of costume. Clothing is also a form of self-expression, and a person wearing a certain style of clothing may or may not ascribe to the clothing's "social message." Each individual bases his or her interpretations of clothing on personal encounters or involvement with discourses such as those mentioned above. Given these circumstances, a universal understanding of the meaning of clothing cannot exist nor can clothing be described by a "continuous, smooth text." Instead, like the discursive formation, the meaning of clothing inhabits what Foucault describes as "a space of multiple dissensions" and contains a "set of different oppositions whose levels and roles must be described."[1]

The overlapping realms of public and private, connecting individual experience with culturally constructed meaning, offer one way to begin examining the interconnections between the various definitions of clothing. For instance, the fact that clothing is at once a cultural symbol and a vehicle of personal expression provides the artists in *Discursive Dress* with an ideal form in which to pursue an *aesthetic* exploration of *political* issues, bringing together two concepts which, until recently, have been understood as opposites. In his article "Beauty Redefined: From Ideal Form to Experiential Meaning," Richard Bolton writes that aesthetics, or the pursuit of ideal form, "implies an autonomous private aesthetic realm of mind where consciousness is sought for its own sake apart from society and community." Political art, on the other hand, embraces certain critical theories which put forward the idea that "all knowledge is social," and calls for "shifting away from ideal form towards the mechanics of publicly derived meaning."[2] The weakness of this dichotomy, which Bolton elaborates on in his essay, has become apparent as more and more artists discover that, by focusing solely on either aesthetics or the political at the expense of the other, their work often results in either purely formal exercises or didactic "one-liners."

In the last few years artists such as those included in *Discursive Dress* have found that combining politics and aesthetics can result in powerful work which engages viewers on several different levels and inspires diverse readings. Each artist discussed here offers his or her perspective on a particular state of our culture and society while simultaneously utilizing the accepted concept that clothing is a personal form of self-expression. Sculpturally abstracting, reconstructing, or recontextualizing clothing, these artists reveal and reexamine social meanings that are implied but not necessarily articulated. At the same time, they manipulate materials, scale, color, weight, and mass to convey personal emotions. There is, however, a self-imposed limit to their alterations: the artists do not abstract the clothing forms beyond recognition. Rather, viewers are given the opportunity to physically and emotionally project themselves into the work, perhaps even to imagine how it would feel and what it would mean to wear these clothes. Consequently, these artists' works give value to the individual in relation to a social context instead of creating a scenario in which the individual is subsumed by the social.

Costume historian Elizabeth Wilson, writing about fashion, states that "fashion displaces emotions into the realm of aesthetics—it is a way of intellectualizing visually about individual desires and social aspirations."[3] In fact, it is evident in the works in *Discursive Dress* that clothing can express contradictory, even irreconcilable, desires and meanings. Through the use of clothing forms, the artists provide for their viewers, to borrow Bolton's words, "well-crafted experiences," not simply formal exercises exploring the construction of clothing or didactic messages espousing their own social/political views, but work which inspires "complex feelings, questions, doubt, and hope."[4] By both revealing how clothing inscribes an individual in the social order and using clothing as a vehicle of personal and aesthetic expression, the artists in *Discursive Dress* map the complexities of both clothing and art.

Subjectivity

Clothing contributes to the construction of human subjectivity. The term subjectivity refers to the numerous structures which make up an individual. These structures, "of which the conscious mind is only a small part" according to literary theorist Toril Moi, "encompass not only unconscious sexual desires, fears, and phobias but also a host of conflicting material, social, political, and ideological factors of which we are equally unaware. It is this highly complex network of conflicting structures . . . that produces the subject and its experiences rather than the other way around."[5] The definition of subjectivity is diametrically opposed to the term "identity" which often describes a seamlessly unified self.

Today clothing is an essential component in the construction of one's subjectivity, subjectivity lying somewhere between clothing and the body. Film theorist Kaja Silverman elaborates:

I would feel impelled to stress as strongly as possible that clothing is a necessary condition of subjectivity—that in articulating the body it simultaneously articulates the psyche. As Freud tells us, the ego is "a mental projection of the surface of the body" and that surface is largely defined through dress. Laplanche makes a similar point when he insists upon the need for an "envelope" or "sack" to contain both "body" and "ego," and to make possible even the most rudimentary distinction between self and other, inside and outside. In effect, clothing is that envelope.[6]

Clothing's role then is to display a unified "identity" while in reality holding together an always fragmented "self." Wilson states that ". . . fashion becomes an important—indeed a vital—medium in the recreation of the lost self or decentered subject."[7] While clothing can often give the appearance of a unified "self," it, like the unconscious, contains contradictory ideas, emotions, and desires, all of which, in both, are turned into symbolic forms. Peter Wollen writes: "Fashion, like the unconscious, does what it wants no matter what. It has even, at every moment, a right of self-contradiction and of taking the opposite side to the decisions it has made the day before."[8] Clothing does not define subjectivity but articulates it, precisely because subjectivity is constantly in flux. Indeed, there are direct parallels between one's steadily changing subjectivity and the continuous flux of fashion.

That one's appearance, which is significantly defined through clothing, is connected to one's definition of "self" is a relatively recent phenomenon. This change occurred in the nineteenth century concurrently with the transition from clothing's function as an indicator of class to that of an indicator of sexual difference. Wilson observes that, in the nineteenth century, appearance and subjectivity became interlinked: "It was the beginning of the idea of the Self as a work of Art, the 'personality' as something that extended to dress, scent, and surroundings, all of which made an essential contribution to the formation of 'self.'"[9] This was, Wilson notes, especially true for women, and she cites Frances Powers Cobbe who wrote in the 1860s:

The more womanly a woman is, the more she is sure to throw her personality over the home and transform it from a mere eating or sleeping place or an upholsterer's showroom, into a sort of outermost garment of her soul; harmonized with all her nature as her robe and the flower in her hair are harmonized with her bodily beauty.[10]

Soon after the shift from clothing as a marker of class to clothing as a marker of gender, dress began to be employed to challenge the dominant bourgeois society's values and beliefs. Wilson identifies the first antibourgeois fashion as dandyism, a style worn by young men in the early nineteenth century adapted from eighteenth-century country and sporting wear.[11] The history of oppositional clothing can be traced from that time forward, through the British Pre-Raphaelites in the mid-nineteenth century, the pre-World War I bohemians who lived in Greenwich Village, proponents of 1940s French existentialism, hippies of the 1960s, British punks of the 1970s, and 1990s members of the Seattle grunge scene, among others. Oppositional clothing, or any clothing for that matter, separates individuals from one another yet also signals the group with whom those individuals affiliate.

Today, clothing continues to function primarily as an indicator of gender. This particular function is important because, as Jane Gaines states, the organization of our society is based on a system of sexual difference which "is guaranteed on a day-to-day basis by gendered dress, adornment, and body style."[12] Just as important is the role of oppositional clothing in challenging gender definitions and boundaries. Oppositional clothing is even more prominent today, for new styles, which often evolve with new music, can be seen regularly on television programming such as MTV. Furthermore, as oppositional clothing is appropriated by high fashion faster than it ever has before, these contestations are accepted and sometimes adopted by the mainstream along with the fashion. For example, androgyny and cross-dressing, while not the norm, are no longer shocking when seen in magazines, fashion shows, or on the street. The frequent play with distinctions between masculinity and femininity through clothing allows for the testing, or trying on, of these new ideas. This "flirting," as Wilson describes it, divests oppositional clothing of its dangers and power.[13] But while some people view the inevitable appropriation of oppositional fashion as a failure of the original act of resistance, Silverman asserts that it is a substantial accomplishment to influence mainstream fashion. She writes: "If . . . clothing not only draws the body so that it can be seen but also maps the shape of the ego, then every transformation within a society's vestimentary code implies some kind of shift within its ways of articulating subjectivity."[14]

For the artists in *Discursive Dress*, clothing becomes a way to chart and examine the many ways we articulate our subjectivity. Gender difference—a main component of subjectivity and a prime source for fashion—is consequently a major issue addressed by these artists. In addition, clothing is commonly a symbol of resistance or opposition to the status quo which prepares the way for these artists to pose their own challenging questions about clothing, the construction of subjectivity, and sexuality. Finally, just as they can count on our ability as viewers to recognize a particular kind of clothing which draws us into the work, these artists can also count on the fact that we have the ability to read clothing symbolically; we look at clothing to reveal significant clues about individuals we meet and interact with on a daily basis.

Naomi London, Elizabeth Leister, Christine LoFaso, and David Eckard all address issues of subjectivity through the use of clothing. Sweaters pinned flat on the wall in Naomi London's *Sweater Project* (cat. no. 13, illus. pp. 20-21) are immediately recognizable as sweaters. In fact, they look very much like the sweaters a mother, grandmother, or close friend might knit; only a loved one takes the time and labor to hand knit a sweater for somebody else today. Yet we cannot help but observe that the sweaters in *Sweater Project* are, for all practical purposes, unwearable. Or rather, we could wear them only if sleeves that hung down to the knees or a turtleneck that encased the head were tolerable.

In her installation, interspersed among the sweaters, London includes black-and-white photographs of elderly women who wear these abstracted sweaters. She commissioned these women, whom she met at a senior citizens center in the Los Angeles area, to fabricate the sweaters for her project. London sees these sweaters as a metaphor for the elderly: "I want to use the metaphor of the nonfunctional garment/sweater as an image of what kind of stigma these people have to carry because of their age."[15] Due to the fact that older people are often viewed as inactive, they are considered useless in a culture that holds one's utilitarianism at a premium. Furthermore, how one makes a living is understood to determine "who you are" including everything from social class to personal temperament. Without the help of this determinant, subjectivity is harder to define, and the uncategorizable are often dismissed in our society. This inability in many of us to find value in some of the other "structures" which contribute to defining who we are as individuals has led many elderly people to feel, in London's words, "nonfunctional—inadequate, physically, emotionally, intellectually, etc."[16] London's nonfunctional sweaters are deliberately constructed to impair either the wearer's mobility or senses and to create a "psychological space" for viewers in which they can empathize with feelings of inadequacy.

Elizabeth Leister's ten-foot-tall wedding dress illustrates how subjectivity exists somewhere between clothing and the body. *Untitled (Wedding Dress)* (cat. no. 9, illus. p. vi) metaphorically represents the mythic proportions of the wedding dress in our culture. The plastic sheeting from which the dress is made suggests artifice—the artifice of the costume, the ritual, perhaps even the institution of marriage itself. Besides pointing to the fetishization of the wedding dress, Leister, who created this work in response to her own experience of getting married, also exhibits the relationship of the wedding dress to women's bodies and subjectivities. The sparkling transparency of Leister's dress replaces the symbolic opaque white of the conventional wedding dress, disclosing the dress' traditional implicit function of announcing the state of the woman's body, her assumed virginity, as she enters into the institution of marriage. Leister's dress makes this historic symbolism explicit, for if one wore Leister's dress, all literally would be exposed. Besides revealing the moral strictures placed on women's bodies, Leister's dress also implies that women's subjectivity has been subsumed by the symbolism of the wedding dress into the role of bride and wife. Through this monumental, transparent dress, Leister releases the woman's body as well as her subjectivity from the matrimonial institution.

Christine LoFaso's *Redress: Gestation Corset and Codpiece* (cat. no. 12, illus. front and back cover) challenges standard definitions of femininity in our culture and embodies resistance to the dominant male order. The work consists of two articles of clothing, the corset and the codpiece, that exemplify the most exaggerated symbols of femininity and masculinity in costume history. A common misconception holds that the corset in the nineteenth century was a universally fashionable and harmful article of clothing. Instead, as art historian David Kunzle argues, "tight-lacing was an expression not of conformity with fashion, which never condoned it, but against conformity with the 'fashionable' (i.e. the culturally dominant) role of the socio-sexually passive maternal woman." Kunzle acknowledges that the corset was a repressive garment but goes on to argue that tight-lacing also had an "expressive and dissident function tending to a kind of female sexual self-assertion, even emancipation."[17]

LoFaso's corset is made from an original nineteenth-century pattern and constructed of paper stained with catnip on which is printed text from Freud's *Dora: An Analysis of a Case of Hysteria.* Decoratively fringed with mink fur, this corset is designed to allow for pregnancy (tight-lacing occasionally was accused of being a means of producing abortion), thus combining the symbol of emancipation with motherhood—two concepts once considered irreconcilable.

The dominant male order, towards which the resistance embodied in LoFaso's work is directed, is present here in the form of Freud's writing and in the codpiece, perhaps the most flagrantly sexual male fashion. Because the corset uses the text *Dora* (a patient of Freud's whom he never succeeded in curing and who finally rejected his treatment), this male dominance is rendered tenuous here. In fact, Toril Moi states that *Dora* "bears all the marks of [Freud's] own fear of losing control and succumbing to the terrifying castrating void exhibited in Dora's hysteria."[18] In this context, the codpiece becomes a symbol of reassurance rather than unfaltering dominance.

As asserted previously, culturally constructed definitions differentiating the sexes have been challenged through experiments in clothing; for instance, the androgynous look and cross-dressing are now integral parts of popular culture. Inventing clothing based on costume history, David Eckard addresses the sexual ambiguity common to our culture today. *Hoop Skirt* (cat. no. 5, illus. p. 17) includes a cloth corset attached to a ribbed hoop skirt of steel, accessories traditionally understood to be used solely by women. But if we refer to costume history, we learn that the corset has been worn by both sexes—for example, tight-lacing of the torso was common in the military during the nineteenth century, particularly in Austria and France. Whereas female tight-lacing was practiced to create a more feminine figure, David Kunzle explains that tight-lacing for males became an athletic or endurance test.[19] The ambiguities embodied by *Hoop Skirt* challenge the way in which we come to conclusions based on simplistic preconceptions about masculinity and femininity. Eckard's work implies that these terms are, in actuality, much more complex, interconnected, and constantly shifting.

The nonfunctional clothing forms in *Discursive Dress* work metaphorically to stall and even halt any conclusive summing up of the notions of subjectivity. These works, like clothing itself, give clues regarding particular meanings, but they always fall short of providing pat definitions, remaining instead deliberately ambiguous.

The Body

In discussing contemporary art which employs clothing but does not depict the body, Richard Martin observes that viewers are given the opportunity to respond to this work "somatically . . . not just aesthetically."[20] The somatic response to an empty dress, that of mentally projecting one's physical self into an article of clothing, suggests the relationship inherent in the body and clothing, a relationship integral to all works in *Discursive Dress*. Kaja Silverman notes, "Dress is one of the most important cultural implements for articulating and territorializing human corporeality—for mapping its erogenous zones, for affixing a sexual identity."[21] Clothing's intimate relationship to the body is why, I would suggest, the artists in *Discursive Dress* have been influenced more by discussions surrounding the body in contemporary art than by artists in earlier decades who incorporated clothing into their work. In fact, the issues surrounding clothing in art can be viewed as an extension of the work currently being done by artists such as Louise Bourgeois, Cindy Sherman, Robert Gober, Kiki Smith, and Rona Pondick who address sexual and political issues using fragmented body parts, disputing the notion that the body is apolitical or an isolated entity separate from culture and society.[22]

Like the body, clothing is intrinsically bound to culture. Therefore, the use of clothing as a vehicle of expression expands upon the work using fragmented body parts because clothing, too, indicates that the human body is more than a biological entity. Elizabeth Wilson writes that clothing links "the biological body to the social being, public to private."[23] Yet the boundary between the body as biological and cultural is unclear, and while clothing functions to link the body to the social world, it also separates the two, indicating this obscure boundary. Wilson suggests, "If the body with its open orifices is itself dangerously ambiguous, then dress, which is an extension of the body yet not quite part of it, not only links that body to the social world, but also more clearly separates the two." This is why, Wilson states, we are drawn to clothing "yet repelled by a fear of what we might find hidden within its purposes."[24]

Wilson's observation that clothing links the body to culture at the same time that it separates the two is similar to what Mario Perniola describes as "transit" or the possibility of movement between clothing and nudity. "Transit," according to Perniola, occurs rarely in the history of figurative art because clothing and nudity instead regularly take on "a primary or essential significance to the exclusion of the other" and consequently become "absolute values." For instance, clothing is understood as a positive state which gives human beings "their anthropological, social, and religious identity, in a word—their being." Nudity, on the other hand, is understood as a "negative state, a privation, loss, dispossession . . . being unclothed meant finding oneself in a degraded and shamed position. . . ."[25] Perniola cites baroque art as an example where "transit" between clothing and nudity was most successful, for instance, in the draped attire of Bernini's *Ecstasy of Saint Theresa* and the anatomical illustrations which depict the body as "a living garment."[26] Yet Perniola does not address why "transit" has not been successful at other times in the history of Western art. Perhaps it is because "transit" deliberately obscures boundaries between the body and clothing, resulting in further blurring of boundaries of culture in both the body and clothing. This concurs with Wilson's thesis: successful "transit" between clothing and nudity makes us uncomfortable specifically because it blurs boundaries and disturbs the order of things—we can no longer identify that which is, in Perniola's terminology, a positive or negative state. Therefore, the relationship between clothing and the body helps to explain the general ambivalence held by our society towards clothing.

The artists in *Discursive Dress* and the artists depicting the fragmented body invert the absolute values associated with clothing and nudity. According to Thomas Laqueur, the work using fragmented body parts demands "the return of pain, sickness, fluids, and meaning of artifacts" to public discourse.[27] In other words, the body is returned to us as part of our "being" and is something to be read or interpreted on a symbolic level. Empty garments, on the other hand, are frequently equated with loss, dispossession, and shame.

Sharon McConnell's *Angel* (cat. no. 14, illus. pp. 22-23) and *Fugitive* (cat. no. 15, illus. p. 22) illustrate the metaphor that clothing is a "second skin," a saying which alludes to clothing's role as an extension of the body. Both *Angel* and *Fugitive* are made from hog gut, which when dried and plied into sheets becomes a delicate, transparent skinlike material. *Angel* is a dress suspended on a hanger hung from the ceiling by a string of gut; it hovers over a rusty metal basin filled with water. The pattern of the dress is based on a simple sleeveless shift with a zipper stitched into the back. Red thread used for the stitched seams alludes to the body's veins running through the skin. *Fugitive*, a billowing robe with full sleeves, contrasts with the more stoic *Angel* and is attached to the wall at the shoulders, displaying the back of this garment of gut. Around the work is a faint but large yellow aureole created with egg yolks painted on the wall. Yellow powder, which McConnell creates by sanding the yolk off the wall, falls on both the garment and the floor.

McConnell's works refer directly to the body, particularly the mortal, fragile body for which her dresses in a sense become shrouds. Like the anatomical illustrations cited by Mario Perniola in which layers of the body are delicately folded back to reveal the internal organs of individuals who look like they are merely sleeping, McConnell's garments are clean and bloodless. But unlike the illustrations, which give no indication of dismemberment, decomposition, or death, McConnell's raiments, in her words, "unavoidably speak of mortality."[28] While they include materials which indicate there was once life—the casings of gut, egg yolks, and red thread which stands in for veins—her dresses focus on death, primarily because of the absence of the body. Death is reinforced in the presentation of the works. *Angel* floats in the air in an almost ghost-like fashion: light shines gently through the transparent dress, making it appear to glow. *Fugitive* is tacked up on the wall like the memento of a missing person which has taken on a life of its own as its yellow luminosity seems to swell and then disintegrate, falling on the garment and the floor. There is a direct link between McConnell's work and the contemporary representation of body parts, both of which sometimes imply a physical violence or at least emphasize the vulnerability of human bodies. A passage written by philosopher Roland Barthes in *The Responsibility of Forms* elucidates the connection: ". . . it is not possible to conceive a garment without the body . . . the empty garment, without head and without limbs . . . is death, not the body's neutral absence, but the body decapitated, mutilated."[29]

In Yong Soon Min's *Remembering Chungshindae* (cat. no. 16, illus. pp. 18-19), the body's absence refers to specific acts of physical violence and oppression towards Korean women. The work consists of a *hanbok*, a traditional Korean dress, which has been stiffened with modeling paste and covered with dirt and pine needles. The skirt is surrounded by a pile of charcoal with more pine needles on the top of the mound. A red light inside the dress shines through small cracks, suggesting smoldering coals.

Remembering Chungshindae specifically memorializes the estimated 200,000 Korean women who were forced to serve as "Military Comfort Troops," i.e., sexual slaves, to Japanese troops all across Asia during World War II.[30] The empty traditional Korean dress symbolizes the wounded, raped bodies of thousands of Korean women but also embodies more than this specific issue. In the Korean countryside, coal and pine boughs are hung at the birth of a baby girl and have come to symbolize the feminine in Korean culture. The dress represents how these physical acts of violence continue to affect Korean women, becoming a part of their shared history. The Korean text by Nora Choi included on the armature of Min's dress and visible at the opening of the neck furthers this idea. The words give voice to the survivors who have been silenced and their grandchildren who have inherited this history. The translation reads as follows:

How much longer will we be forced to sacrifice?
How long will we be silenced?
How much of our body is our own?
When will our spirits be able to rest?

The text continues on the skirt:

Grandmother, please live for a long time.
Grandmother, please make us remember.
As history's witness, live forever.
We will not be fooled again.[31]

Michele Blondel's *Concue. . .Baptisee. . .Communiante* (cat. no. 1, illus. p. 24) exemplifies the inversion of the absolute values associated with clothing and nudity. She includes both empty dresses and fragmented body parts in this work to address the visibility and the invisibility of the body in the philosophy and art of the Catholic Church. Blondel, who was born and raised Catholic in France, has explored during the last couple of years the contradictions of her faith through her art, especially contradictions regarding sexuality. She relates how, as a child, she was particularly moved by the sensual religious art decorating French cathedrals and perplexed at the same time by the teachings of her church which never spoke about the sensuality of the body so evident in the art.

In *Concue. . .Baptisee. . .Communiante,* three sheer white cotton dresses worn by Blondel on the days of her birth, baptism, and First Communion hang from three sections of a large triangular iron armature. A womb-shaped vessel rests on the floor beneath each of the three dresses; hanging from a metal rod on either side of the dresses are two phallic shapes. All five body shapes are made from Baccarat crystal. By utilizing such a precious material, Blondel draws attention to reproductive organs in a manner that would be unlikely in the Catholic Church. When compared to the voluptuous body parts, the dresses look like fragile relics. Rather than celebrating "pureness," as the white garments originally symbolized, these dresses now forecast the ensuing and inevitable shame of the wearer.

Maureen Connor's *Thinner Than You* (cat. no. 2, illus. p. 26) and *Untitled* (cat. no. 4, illus. p. 27) link the body and clothing to culture. *Thinner Than You* consists of a black, slightly transparent, sliplike, mesh dress hanging taut on a metal clothing display stand. The waist of the dress is twisted around the single rod of the stand to create the illusion of an unnaturally thin waist. *Untitled*, which works in tandem with *Thinner Than You,* is its opposite. A body suit made from the same material is stretched over a round convex mirror that hangs suspended by thick rubber cords and is braced from below by four gracefully curved metal supports.

These works specifically address the lack of distinction made between women and their clothes in our culture. Together women and their clothes are understood to represent "femininity." In turn, fashionable clothes determine fashionable body shapes and sizes. Kaja Silverman writes: "Clothing exercises . . . [a] profoundly determining influence upon living breathing bodies . . . affecting contour, weight, muscle development, posture, movement, and libidinal circulation."[32] This is evident in the use by women in the past of corsets, bustles, and hoops to obtain the popular shape. Today these accessories have been replaced by diets and exercise, phenomena that Connor directly addresses in *Thinner Than You* and *Untitled*. Her sculptures critique society's proclivity to meld "femininity" and appearance, and they refer directly to the extreme consequences of the current fitness and slimming mania—anorexia and bulimia.

The body is decontextualized in a similar manner in all the works in *Discursive Dress*: the whole body is missing. But while the physical body might be missing, it is, significantly, *not* absent. Rather, the body is implicit in all the works in *Discursive Dress*, and, despite the abstractions or recontextualizations, each article of clothing maintains the physical capacity to hold the shape and form of a body (if not without some discomfort). The physical representation of the body has not been left out of these works as an act of resistance towards the way it has been represented in the past. Instead, the void is employed to provide a space for the pursuit of new readings and explorations of the body which challenge the concept that only one universal theory about the body can exist.

Fantasy

The enigmatic and shifting relationships among clothing, the body, the psyche, our subjectivities, and society open up a space for the expression of fantasy and imagination. Fantasy allows for explorations of desire and necessarily concedes to contradictions, which open up paths for innovation. Fantasy also contributes to the previous discussion regarding subjectivity: it provides an impetus to investigate new subjectivities, including the crossing of gender boundaries.

Cora Kaplan expounds on the complexities of fantasy in her essay, "The Thorn Birds: Fiction, Fantasy, Femininity." She explains that fantasy is not simply "a conscious construction of an imaginary scene" but the exploration and production of "desires which may be in excess of the socially possible or acceptable."[33] Her explanation, based on Freudian psychoanalysis, identifies fantasy as a continuous process which can express social content but at the same time is separate from it. Kaplan elaborates on this theory by referring to psychoanalyst Juliet Mitchell's discussion of the origin of fantasy:

[Fantasy's] . . . moment of genesis [is] the moment when the baby deprived of the breast fantasizes sucking, transforming the external world and its "things"—the people, sounds, sights, and smells and so on, into representation. This moment is identified in psychoanalysis as the moment of the foundation of desire and, according to Mitchell again, as the moment when the "human animal" becomes a "human being." Thus the experiences of the external world provide the support (or underpin) for the fantasy scenario which comes into being with their absence.[34]

Clothing, like fantasy, captures our imagination and allows us to explore alternatives: it opens up a space for invention. Clothing's ambiguity and our general ambivalence towards clothing make possible, in Julia Kristeva's words, "the liberation of the imaginary."[35] Because clothing draws on unconscious fantasy, it represents the way expression moves from the inner psyche to the larger world. "Hence," writes Elizabeth Wilson, fashion's "compulsiveness, hence our ambivalence, hence the immense psychological (and material) work that goes into the production of the social self, of which clothes are an indispensable part."[36] Both fashion and fantasy, particularly the Harlequin and Gothic romances that Cora Kaplan discusses, are shunned, often by feminists, as interests that are "incorrect." Both fashion and fantasy, it has been argued, pander to the oppressive male-dominated order where women are taught to appraise themselves through perspectives held by men. This results in women being considered intellectually inferior, reduced to possessions and objects of desire. But it is in both clothing and fantasy that the possibility of resistance has been identified. Wilson observes: "The pointlessness of fashion is precisely what makes it valuable. It is in this marginalized area of the contingent, the decorative, the futile, that not simply a new aesthetic but a new cultural order may seed itself."[37] Similarly, Cora Kaplan observes that "Fantasy . . . has utopian elements in it; indeed, without fantasy we could not imagine utopias."[38]

Pamela Keech's installation *Lust & Etiquette* (cat. no. 8, illus. pp. 32-34) draws us into an arena of pure fantasy based on the seventeenth-century salon. Seven figures inhabit the installation, all wearing period-type costumes designed and sewn by Keech. The figures, some of which have rakes, candles, or bird cages for heads and synthetic hair fashioned in long curls for hands, act out romantic vignettes. Each item in the installation has a specific meaning, based on a symbolic system familiar to the broad public during the baroque period, which furthers the narrative. For instance, a pruning hook represents the severing of a liaison, and the stub of an extinguished candle signifies the end of burning desire. A written key explains what each of the objects in the installation means, thus providing the opportunity for the story to unravel as we recognize the clues.

The setting, the objects, the figures' poses, and their clothing are the instigators of this narrative; a story takes place in front of us regardless of whether or not we use the key. In short, it is not words, actions, or knowledge of the baroque period but rather the setting, clothing, and other visual clues which take over our imagination. Kaplan quotes J. Laplanche and J.-B. Pontalis who state: "Fantasy is not the object of desire but its setting. In fantasy, the subject does not pursue the object or its sign, he appears caught up himself in the sequence of images."[39]

Cameron Shaw's art suggests alternative ways of containing history. *Refuge #28* (cat. no. 18, illus. p. 31), *Untitled Open Box with Washington's Letter and Three Shirts* (cat. no. 19), *Untitled Box with White Panel Five Infant Shirts and Twelve Adult Shirts* (cat. no. 17, illus. p. 30), and *Untitled Stack with Katzenjammer Kids and Blue Shirt* (cat. no. 20) are carriers of incomplete, fragmented histories including comic strips, letters written by our "forefathers," newspapers ("daily myth makers," according to Shaw), and men's shirts. Each of the boxes is covered with herringbone wool, a material commonly used for men's suits which Shaw has saturated in beeswax. The herringbone fabric and the standard men's shirts—a product of "The Great Masculine Renunciation" when, in the nineteenth century, men's clothing became simplified and adapted to the needs of labor—stand in for the historically male-dominated order of our society. Shaw also sees the shirts as representing facets of the life cycle. For instance, *Untitled Box with White Panel Five Infant Shirts and Twelve Adult Shirts* contains infant shirts which the viewer cannot see because they are in the closed box. The invisible white infant shirts represent the state of being "unstained," or "unblemished," as a child, of "starting out clean," presumably a state that will change as one enters into maturity and the adult world.[40] Furthermore, because we cannot see these particular shirts, they can connote either the next generation or the memory of those past. While these notions are more psychological than those investigated by most historians, they are, nonetheless, directly related to history. In fact, they imply that history is much more complicated than the compact and linear version, dominated by individual men and their wars, that is often presented to us. Through his work, Shaw displays history as an ambiguous amalgam of facts and fictions, that is negotiated, revised, and transformed by individuals for their own purposes.

Allan Wexler's works exemplify one way clothing can be used to create a new space and suggest the possibility of a new cultural order. In *Four White Shirts Sewn into a Tablecloth* (cat. no. 21) and *Four Shirt Collars Sewn into a Tablecloth* (cat. no. 22, illus. p. 25), Wexler creates a utopian alternative for the organization, function, and interaction around a daily ritual, sitting at the table for a meal. Wexler, an architect by training, has been using the table-and-chair format for fifteen years. He sees the table and chairs, which symbolically represent the center of family life, as "social and ritual building units" with which he explores how function and ritual mutually inform each other.[41] Here Wexler extends this examination to the table covering itself. In *Four White Shirts Sewn into a Tablecloth*, the tails of four men's shirts are sewn on to each side of a square tablecloth. The tablecloth and each shirt are then stretched out and mounted flat on the wall. *Four Shirt Collars Sewn into a Tablecloth* is just that and is displayed in the same manner described above. By making shirts and collars integral to the tablecloth, suggesting one or the other must be "worn" to participate at the table, Wexler provides the opportunity to think about modes of human interaction and how these behaviors are affected by physical configurations. His choice of white shirts and collars to explore this situation visually draws attention to the conflicting issues of equality and conformity. The white shirts could represent equality—all four people in this situation could be equal—or conformity—because white shirts have been more or less a uniform for men, they could here indicate that the choice of participation was not theirs. Whether Wexler is presenting us with a small scale utopia for the everyday or a situation of forced participation and interaction is left up to the viewer. Regardless, Wexler, like Keech, Shaw, and the other artists in *Discursive Dress*, opens up the possibility for alternatives to the way things are viewed or done, which, in turn, reveals possibilities for social change.

Conclusion

Our fascination with clothing is linked to our ambivalence towards it. Clothing articulates aspects of the conflicting structures which make up our subjectivities. It cloaks our nakedness so that we do not have to confront our physical bodies. Yet, dress is employed perhaps more than any other symbolic system in our society to announce our sexuality. It motivates our fantasies, providing us with the opportunity to express contradictory desires and explore beyond social conventions. Clothing can reassure us when it exists comfortably in the order of things, or it can threaten to disrupt this order. Clothing's meanings are fickle; they can go one way or the other, any time, any place.

Ultimately, clothing's meanings remain in flux because the structures they are attached to are constantly transforming and realigning themselves. Consequently, our understanding of clothing always includes ambiguities. These ambiguities empower the works in *Discursive Dress*, allowing them to be read in assorted ways and on numerous levels, many more than the ones offered here. This particular aspect of clothing may explain its prolific use as a vehicle of expression in contemporary art today. Artists can put forth their own positions, agendas, feelings, and emotions but can count on, to some degree, clothing's ambiguities to prevent didacticism. On the other hand, by using familiar forms, the use of clothing engages viewers and encourages readings based on personal experiences and associations. The purpose of these clothing forms, like Foucault's notions of discourse, is to make differences, cultivate connotations, and maintain irregularities and movements back and forth. In this context, the dichotomies which organize so much of our thinking break down and allow fashion and clothing to become *Discursive Dress*.

ENDNOTES

1 Michel Foucault, *The Archaeology of Knowledge* (New York: Pantheon Books, 1972), 155.

2 Richard Bolton, "Beauty Redefined: From Ideal Form to Experiential Meaning," *New Art Examiner* (November 1993), 27-28.

3 Elizabeth Wilson, *Adorned in Dreams: Fashion and Modernity* (London: Virago, 1985), 9.

4 Bolton, 27, 31.

5 Toril Moi, *Sexual/Textual Politics: Feminist Literary Theory* (London and New York: Routledge, 1985), 10.

6 Kaja Silverman, "Fragments of a Fashionable Discourse," *Studies in Entertainment: Critical Approaches to Mass Culture*, Tania Modleski, ed. (Bloomington and Indianapolis: Indiana University Press, 1986), 147.

7 Wilson, 122.

8 Peter Wollen, "Fashion/Orientalism/The Body," *New Formations* Volume 1 (Spring 1987), 29.

9 Wilson, 123.

10 Ibid.

11 Ibid., 180.

12 Jane Gaines, "Introduction: Fabricating the Female Body," *Fabrications: Costume and the Female Body*, Jane Gaines and Charlotte Herzog, eds. (New York and London: Routledge, 1990), 26.

13 Wilson, 122.

14 Silverman, 149.

15 Quoted in James D. Campbell, "Corporeal Yarns: Body and Privation in the Art of Naomi London," *Naomi London* (Montreal, Quebec: Galerie Samuel Lallouz, 1992), 7.

16 Ibid., 6-7.

17 David Kunzle, *Fashion and Fetishism: A Social History of the Corset, Tight-Lacing and Other Forms of Body-Sculpture in the West* (Totowa, New Jersey: Rowman and Littlefield, 1982), xvii-xviii.

18 Moi, 135.

19 Kunzle, 112-117.

20 Richard Martin, "Approximating the Body," *New Art Examiner* (September 1993), 17.

21 Silverman, 146.

22 The exhibition and catalogue which best address the phenomenon of artists using fragmented body parts is *Corporal Politics* curated by Helaine Posner at the MIT Visual Arts Center.

23 Wilson, 2-3.

24 Ibid., 246-247.

25 Mario Perniola, "Between Clothing and Nudity," *Fragments for a History of the Human Body*, Part Two, Michel Feher with Ramona Naddaff and Nadia Tazi, eds. (New York: Urzone, 1989), 237.

26 Ibid., 253.

27 Thomas Laqueur, "Clio Looks at Corporal Politics," *Corporal Politics* (Cambridge and Boston: MIT List Visual Arts Center and Beacon Press, 1992), 15.

28 Sharon McConnell, "Artist's statement," *Visiting Artists* brochure, 3 February-10 March 1993 (The Iris and B. Gerald Cantor Art Gallery, College of the Holy Cross, Worcester, Massachusetts).

29 Roland Barthes, *The Responsibility of Forms* (New York: Farrar, Strauss and Giroux, 1985), 107.

30 According to a press release distributed by the Korean Working Group in New York City, *Chungshindae* were forced to live in appalling conditions and were frequently raped, beaten, drugged, and killed. This issue has been all but forgotten, hidden for years by both the survivors, whose shame kept them from coming forward, and the Japanese government. The press release states that the survivors have received only an ambiguous apology and no restitution from the government.

31 Translated in Yong Soon Min's unpublished artist's statement.

[32] Silverman, 146.

[33] Cora Kaplan, "The Thorn Birds: Fiction, Fantasy, Femininity," *Formations of Fantasy*, Victor Burgin, James Donald, and Cora Kaplan, eds. (London: Methuen and Co. Ltd., 1986), 149.

[34] Ibid.

[35] Julia Kristeva, "Histoires d'Amour," *Desire*, Lisa Appignanesi, ed. (London: Institute of Contemporary Art, 1983), 21.

[36] Wilson, 246.

[37] Ibid., 245.

[38] Kaplan, 153.

[39] Ibid.

[40] Cameron Shaw, interview by Curator of Exhibitions Alison Ferris, telephone conversation, Sheboygan, Wisconsin, December 1992.

[41] Lynn Breslin, "View From the Tea House: Allan Wexler's Transformation Scenes," *Elle Decor* (September 1990), 42.

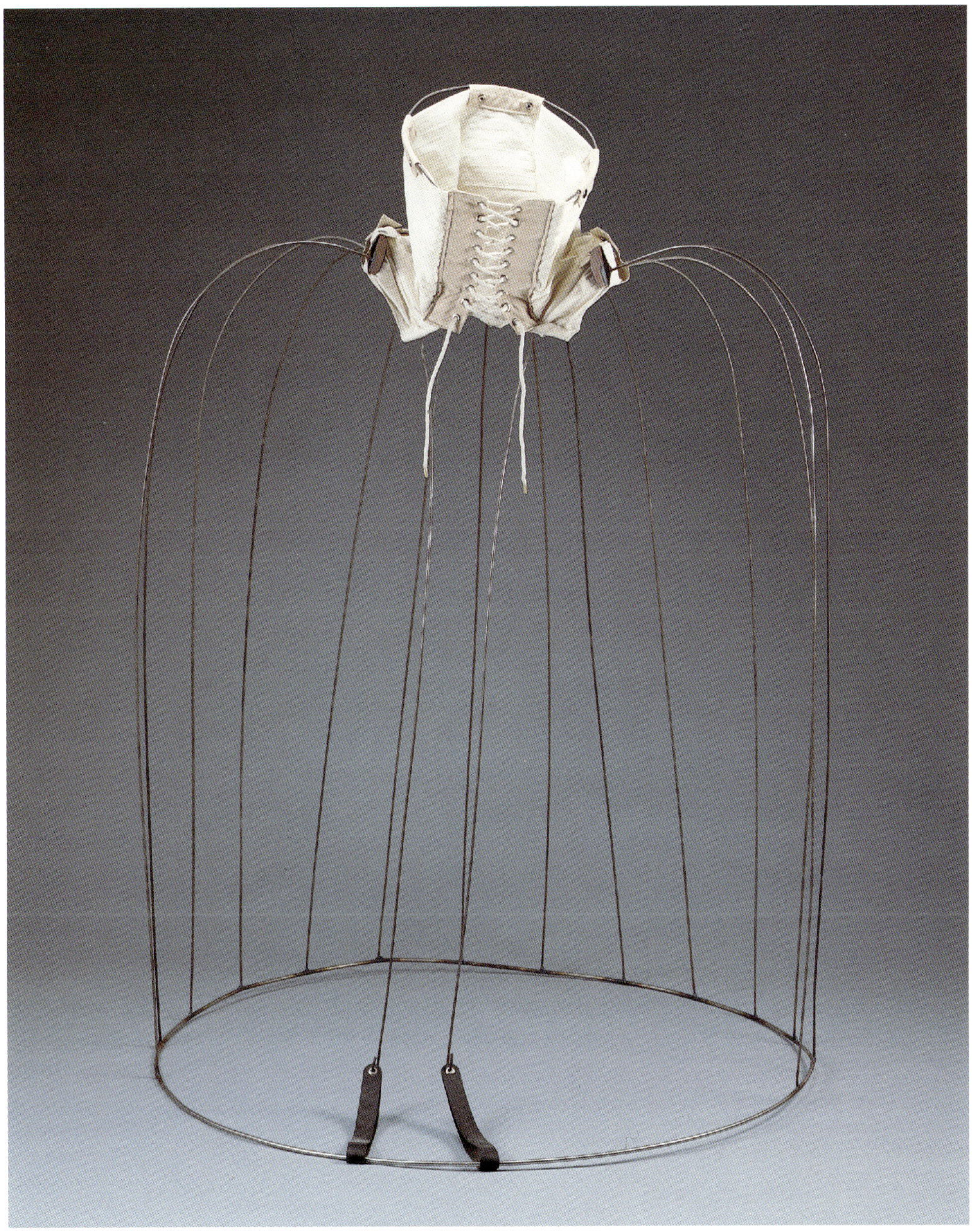

David Eckard, *Hoop Skirt*, 1992, 61¼ x 42 x 40¾"

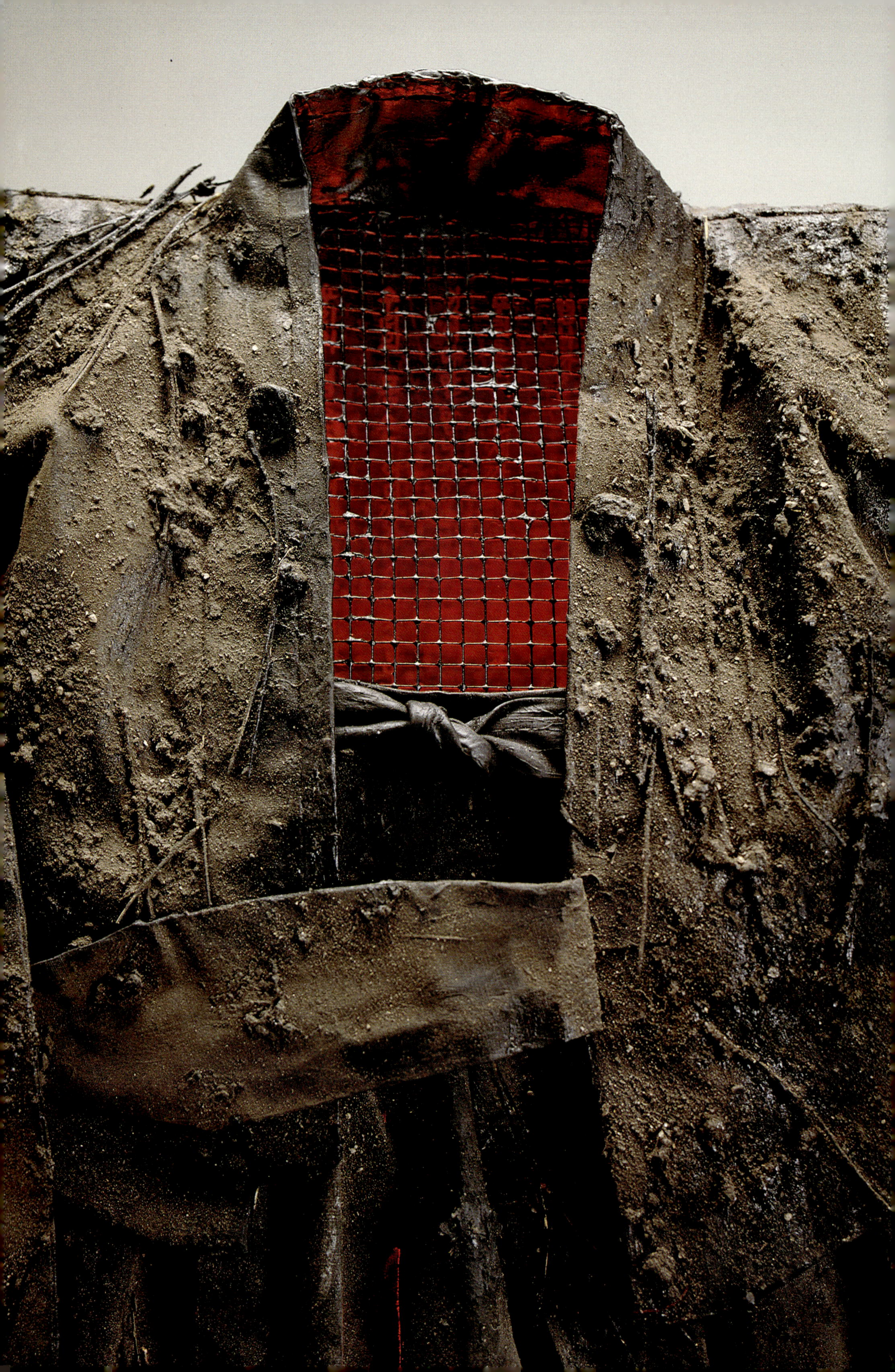

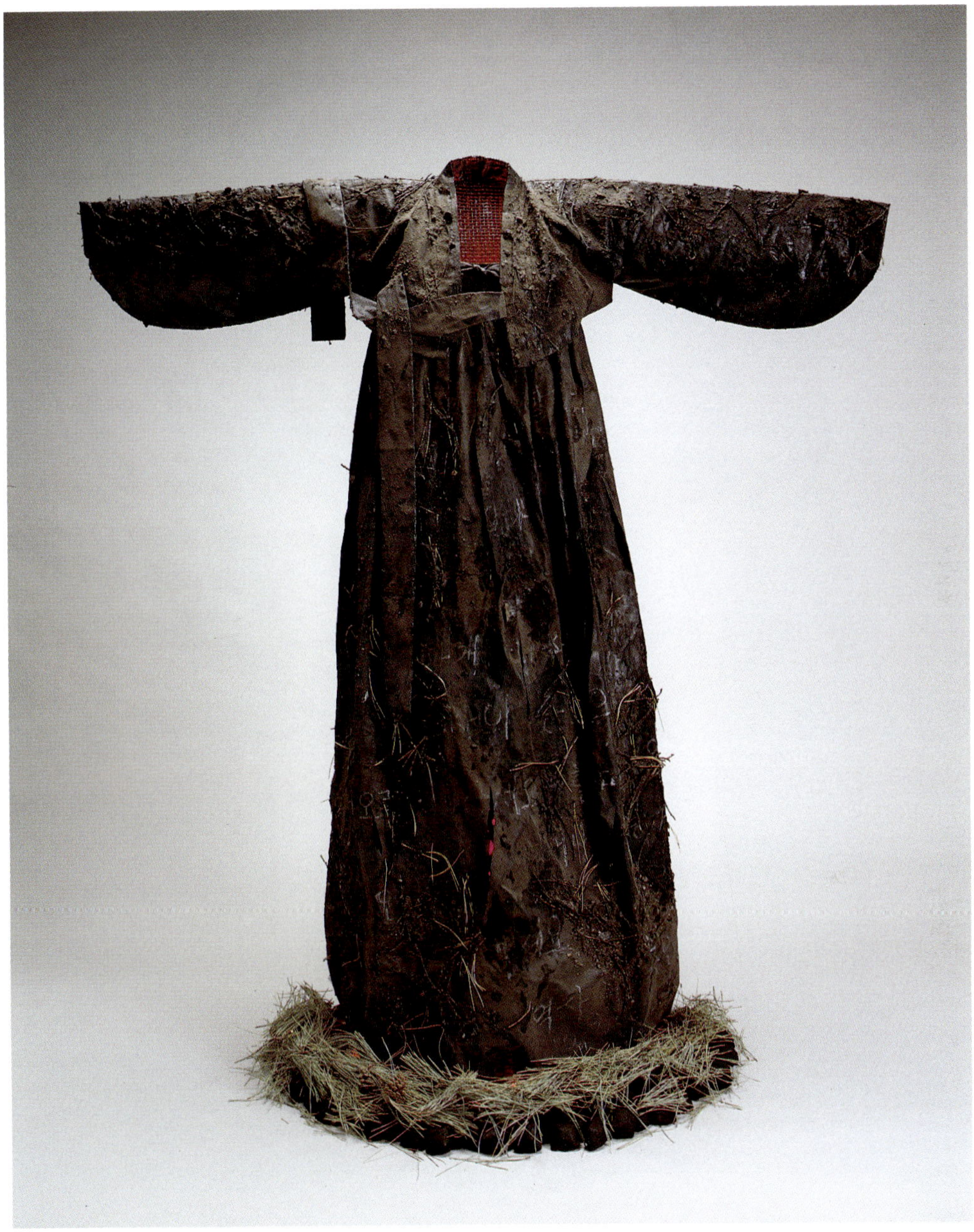

Above: Yong Soon Min, *Remembering Chungshindae*, 1992, 62½ x 55 x 31"

Left: *Remembering Chungshindae*, detail

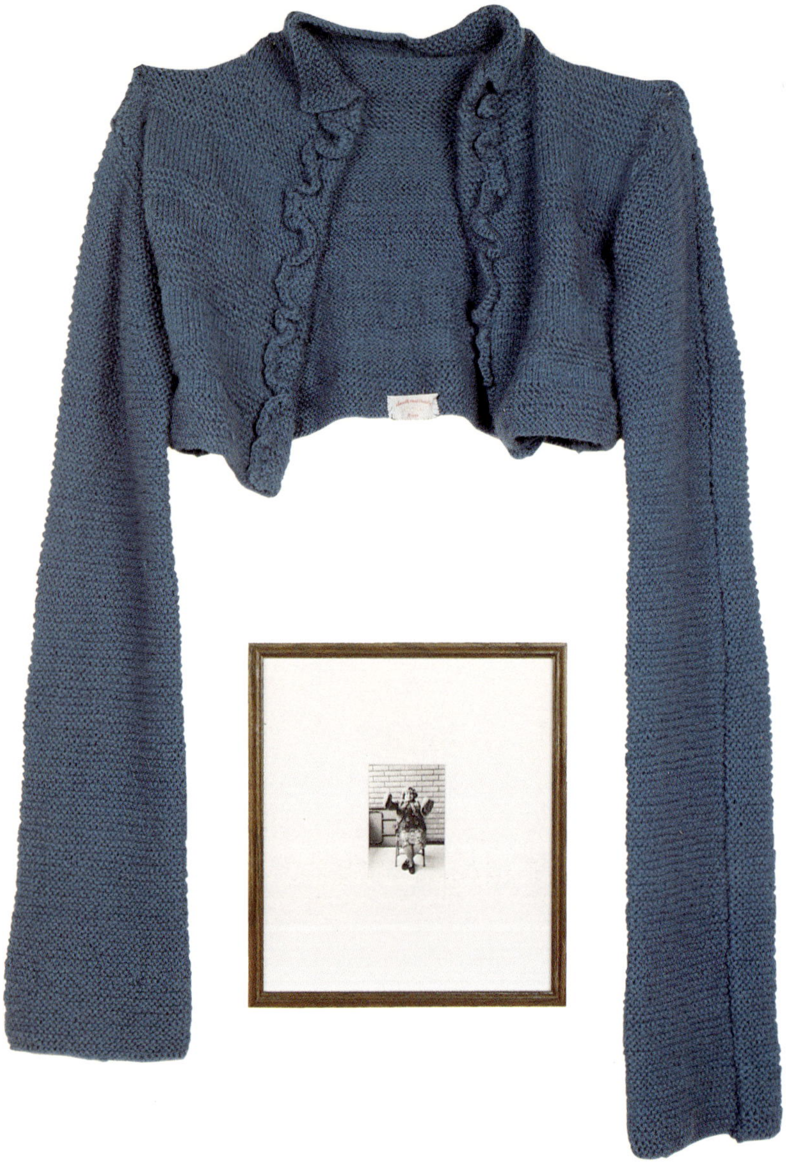

Above: Naomi London, *The Sweater Project*, detail, 1991-92, 131 x 183 x 5"

Right: *The Sweater Project*, detail

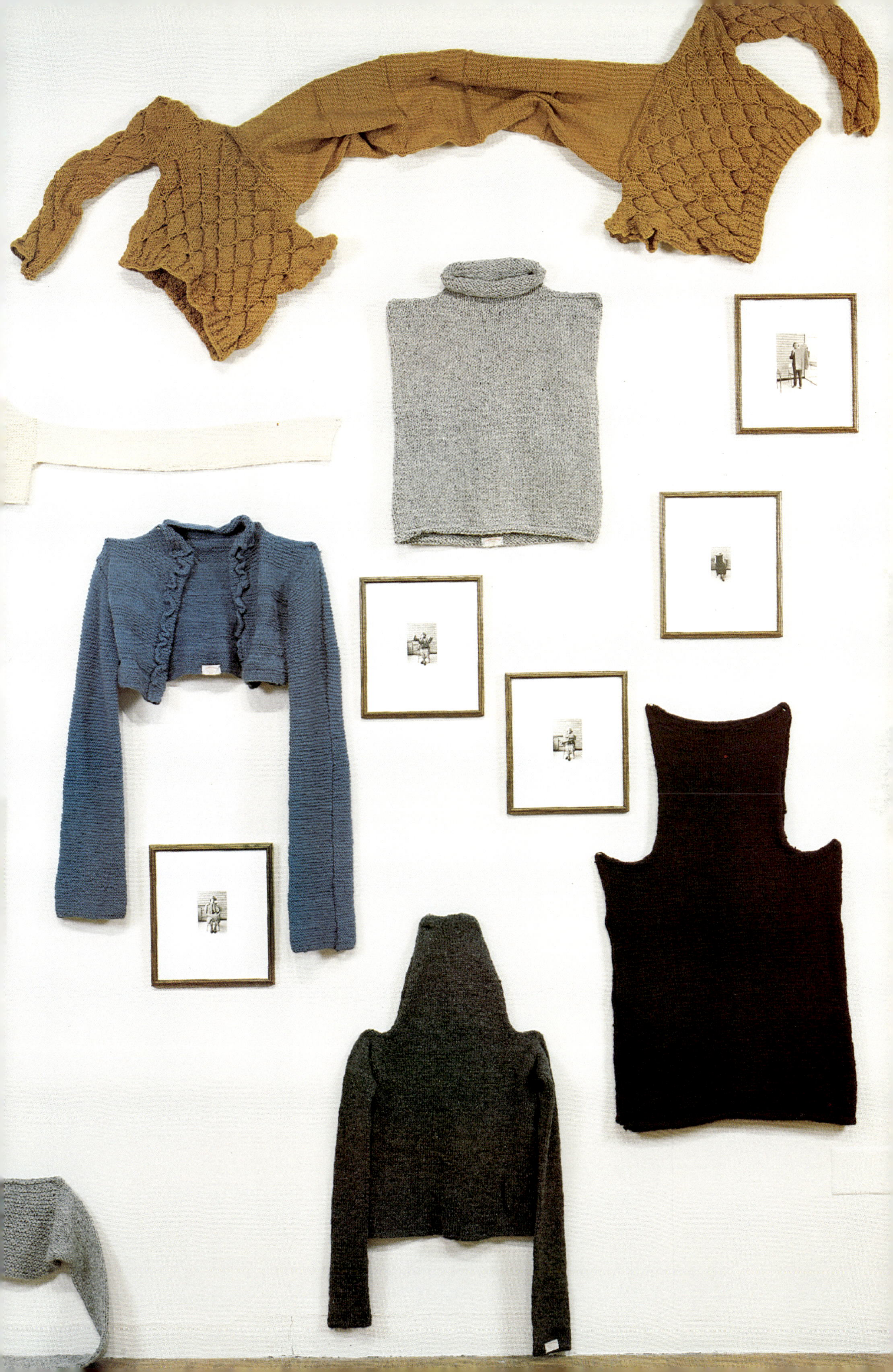

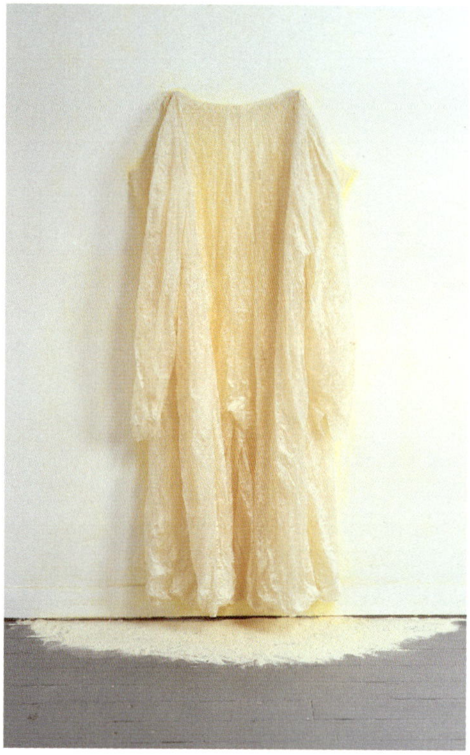

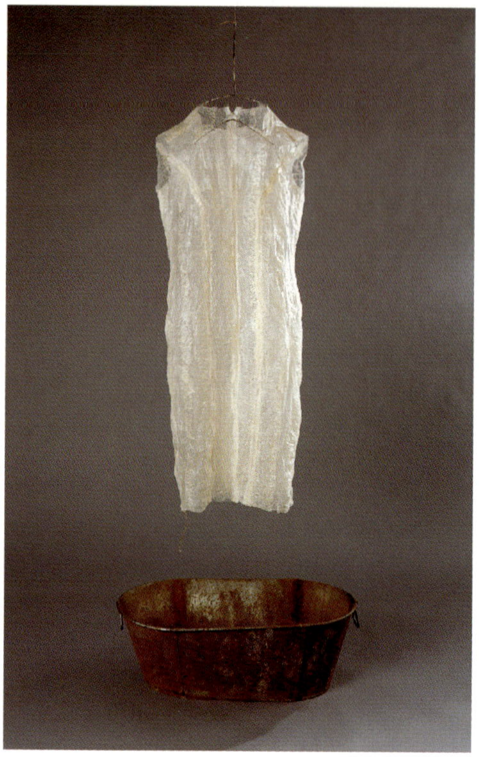

Above Left: Sharon McConnell, *Fugitive*, 1992-93, 108 x 78 x 4¼"

Above Right: Sharon McConnell, *Angel*, 1991, 68 x 25¾ x 14"

Right: *Angel*, detail

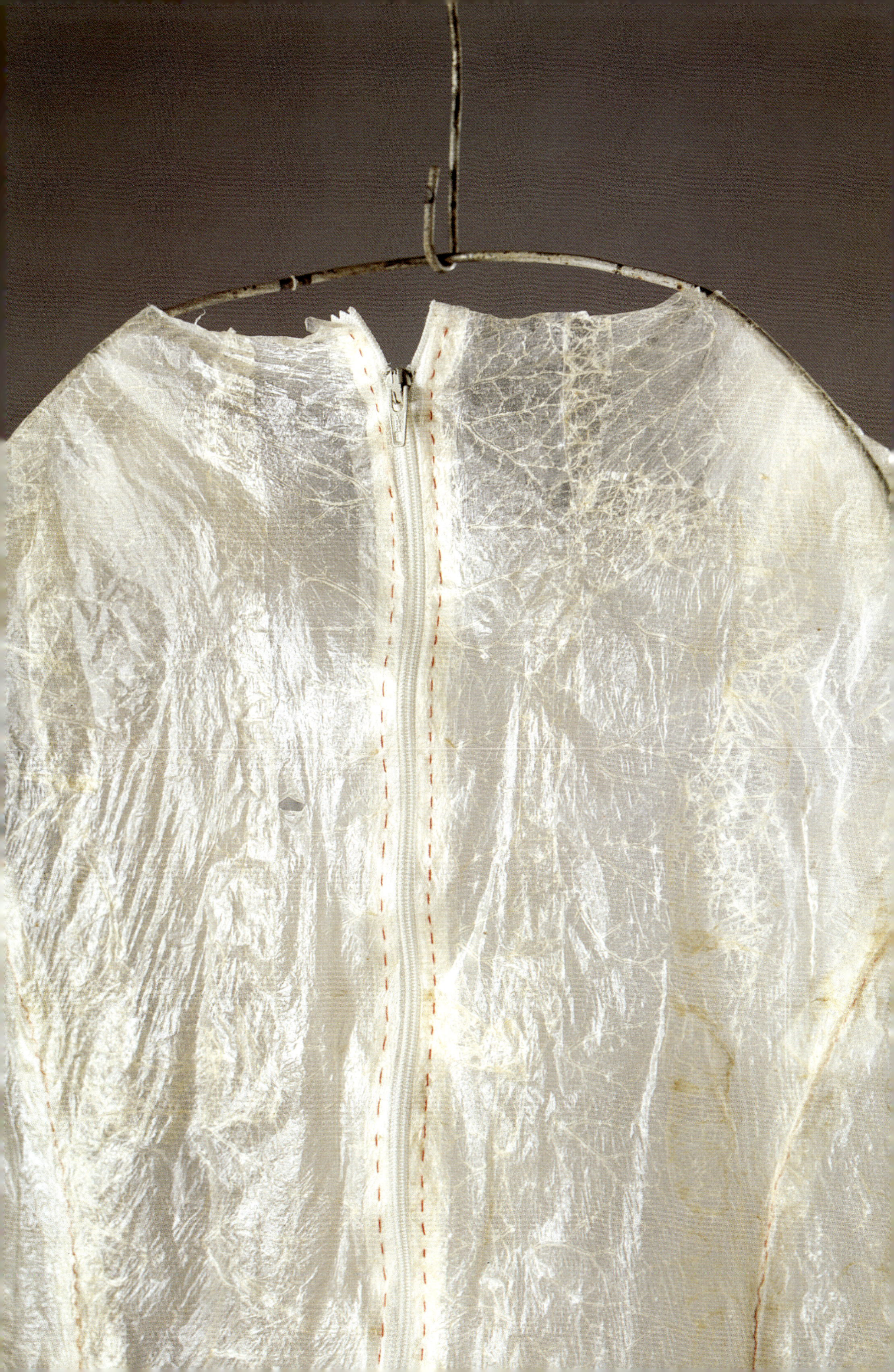

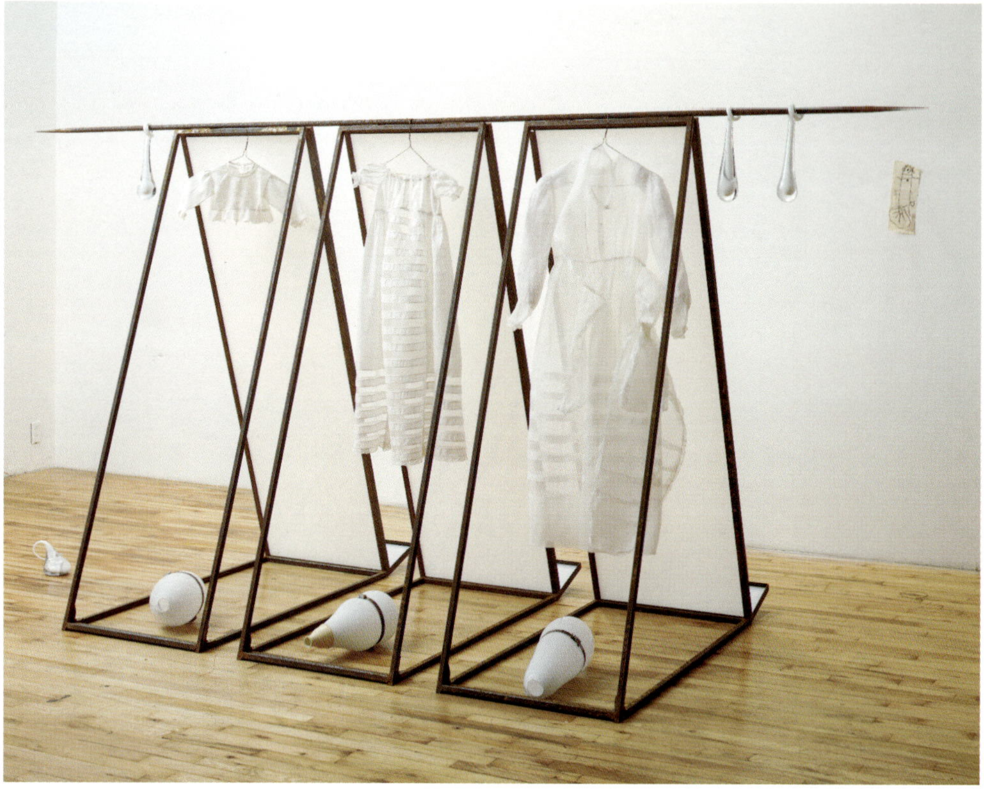

Michele Blondel, *Concue...Baptisee...Communiante*, 1987, 69 x 142¼ x 56"

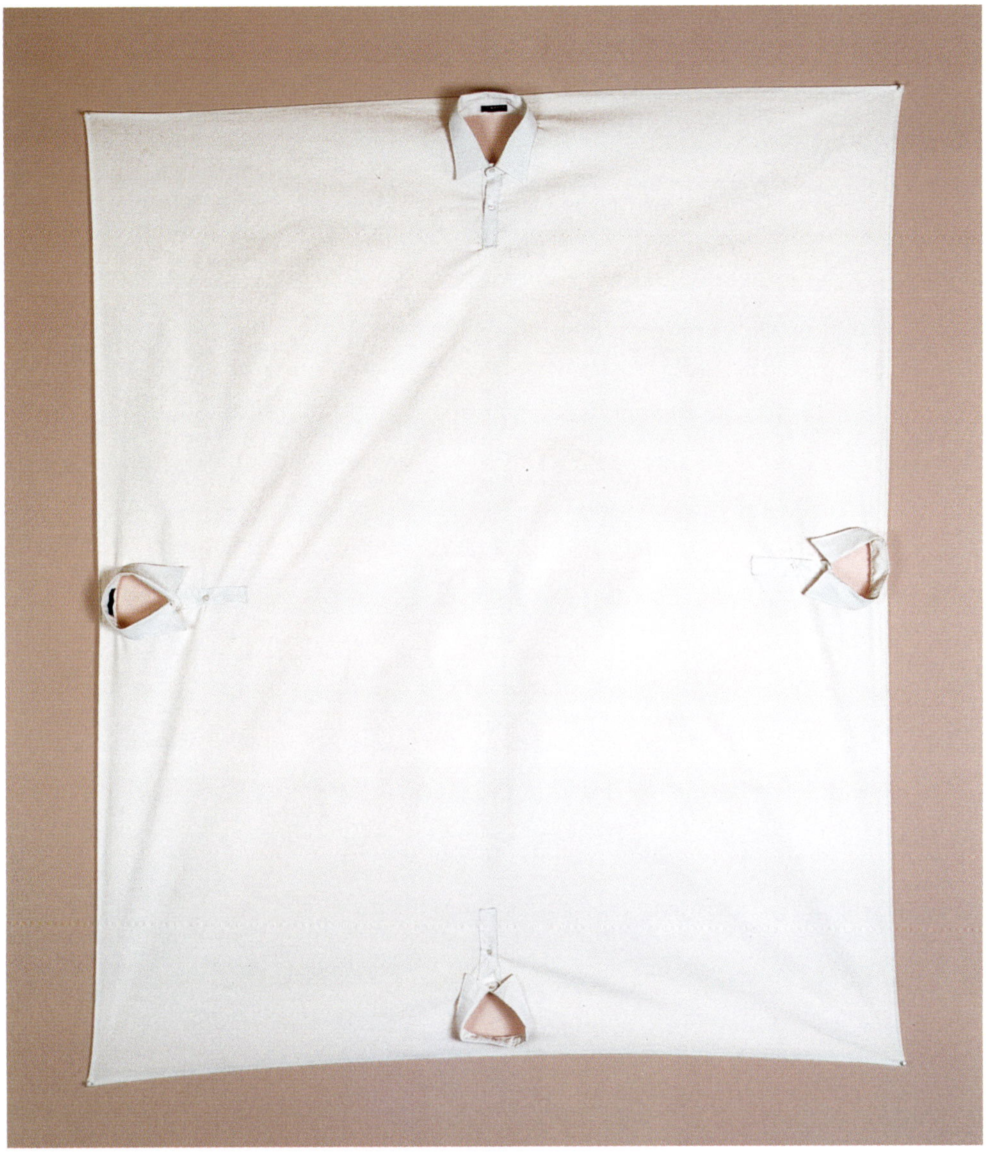

Allan Wexler, *Four Shirt Collars Sewn into a Tablecloth*, 1991, 71 x 62 x 2"

Next Page: Maureen Connor, *Thinner Than You*, 1990, 60 x 15 x 7½"

Following Page: Maureen Connor, *Untitled*, 1990, 132½ x 42¼ x 42¼"

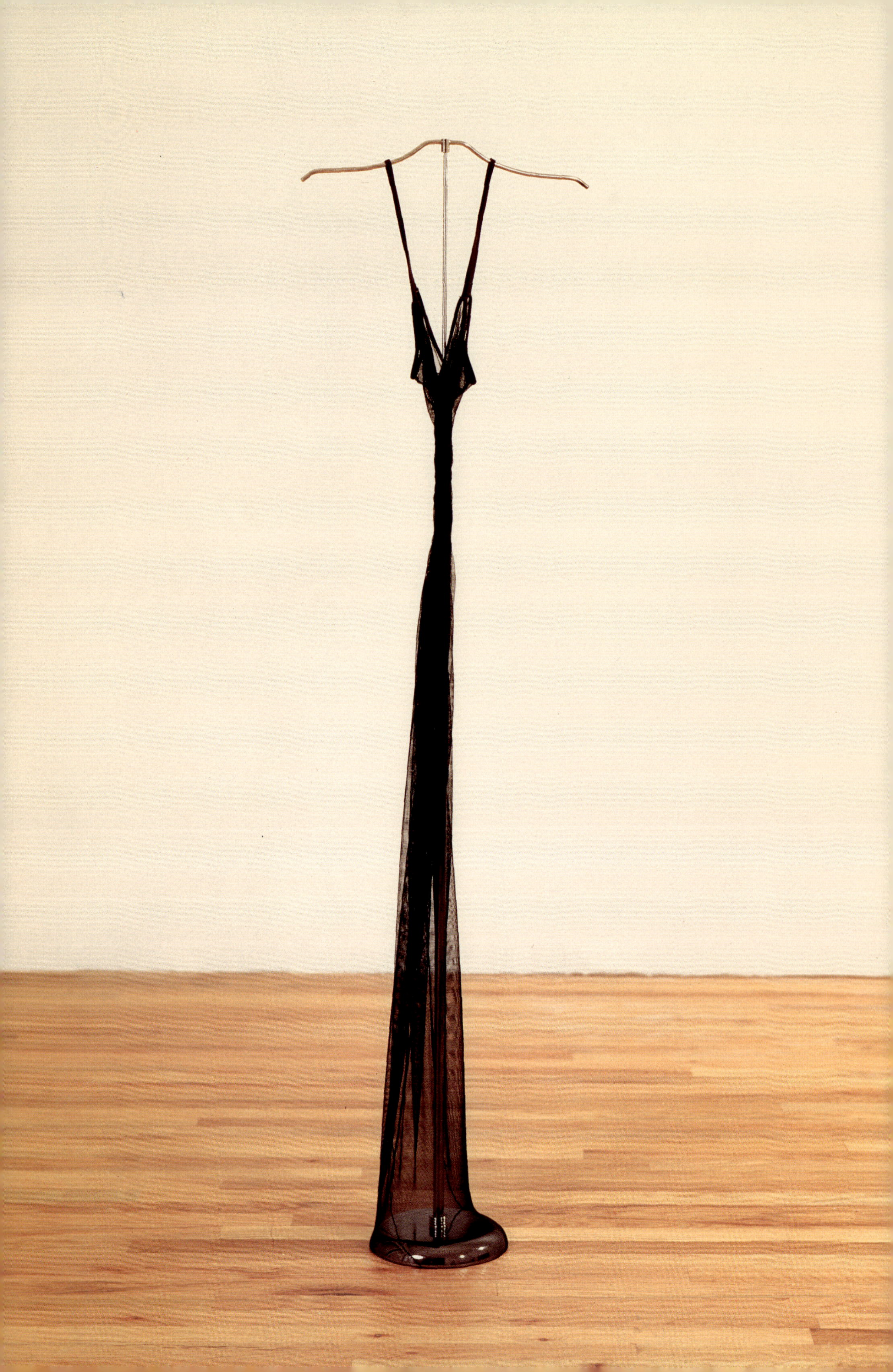

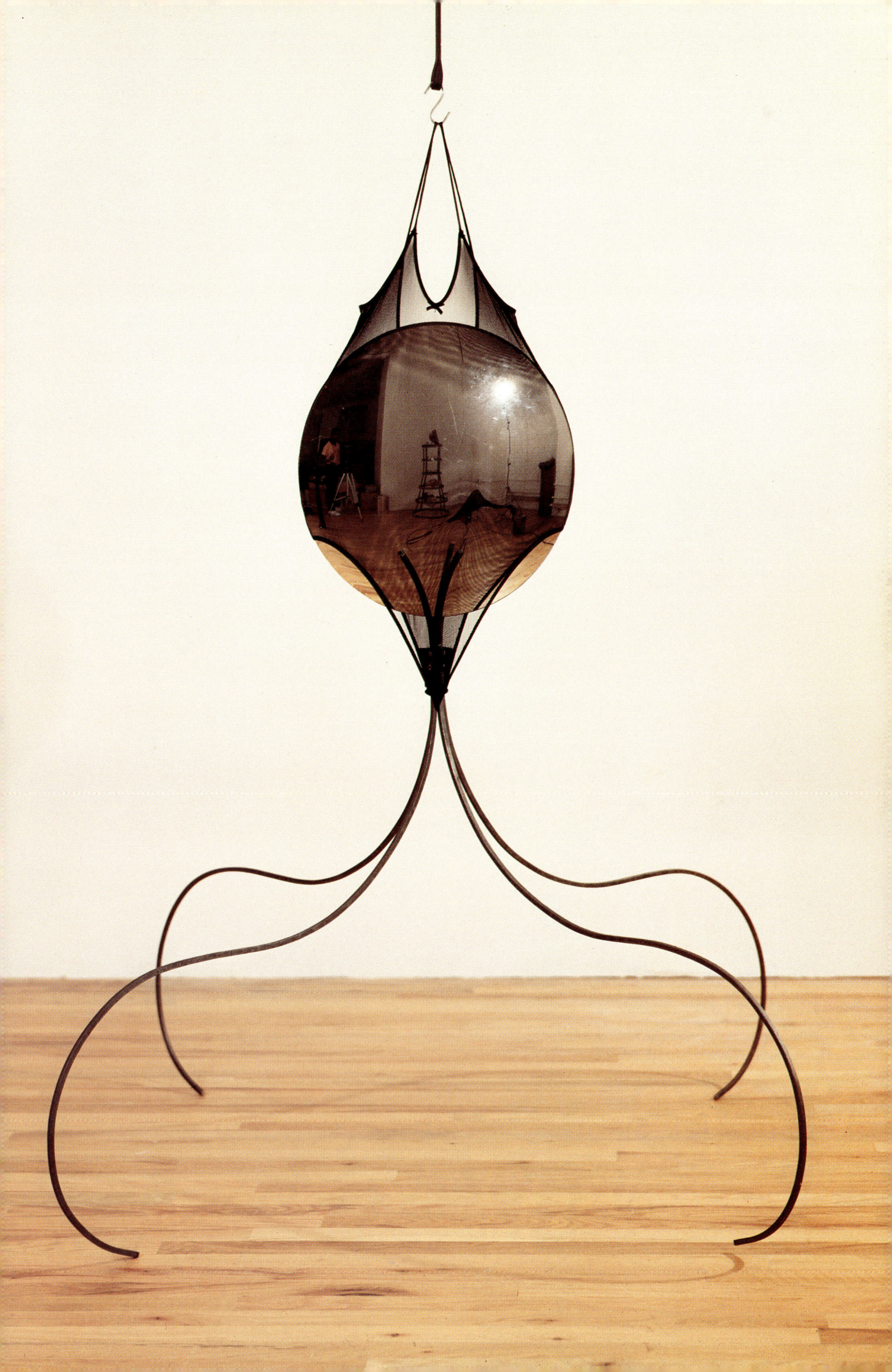

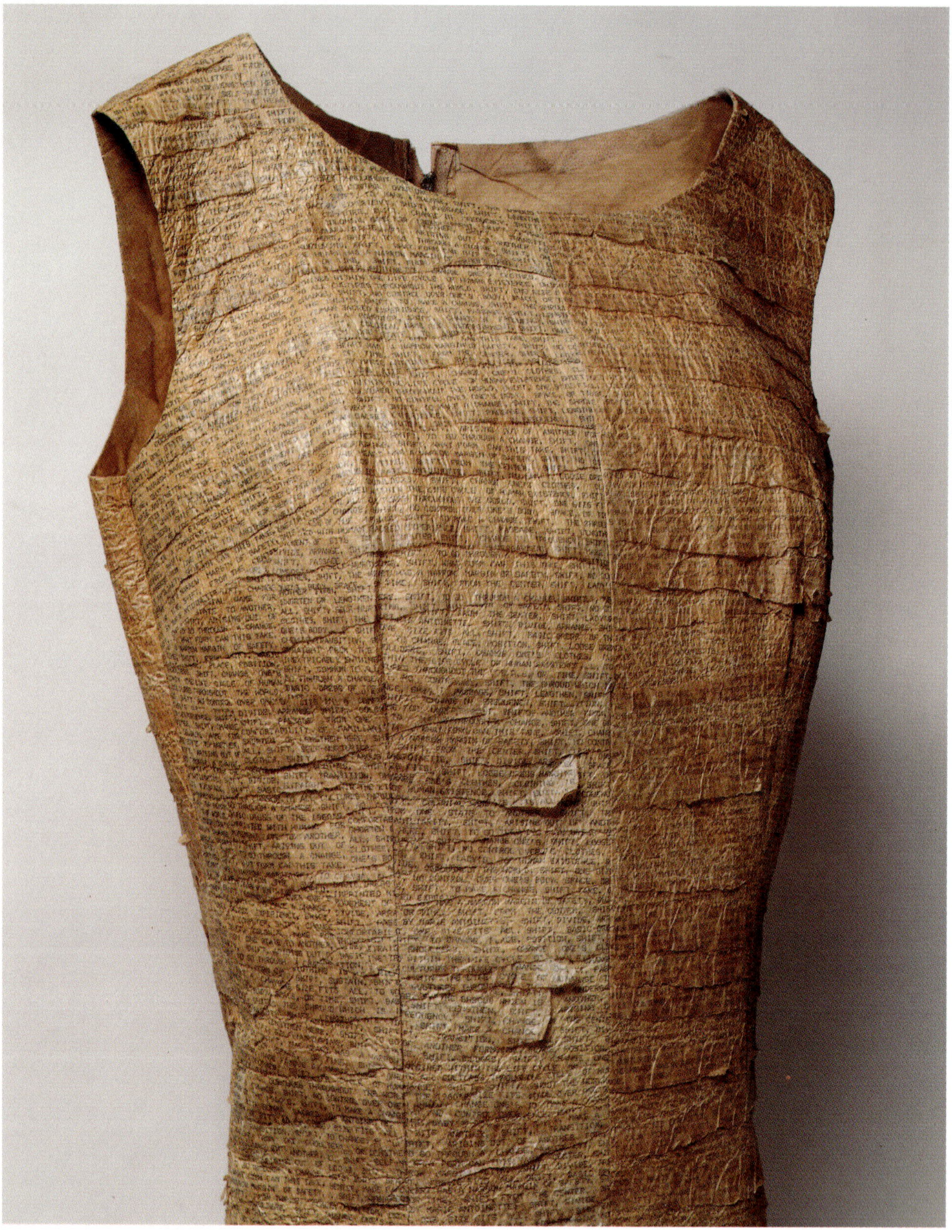

Right: Christine LoFaso, *Shift*, 1992, 88 x 21 x 11"

Above: *Shift*, detail

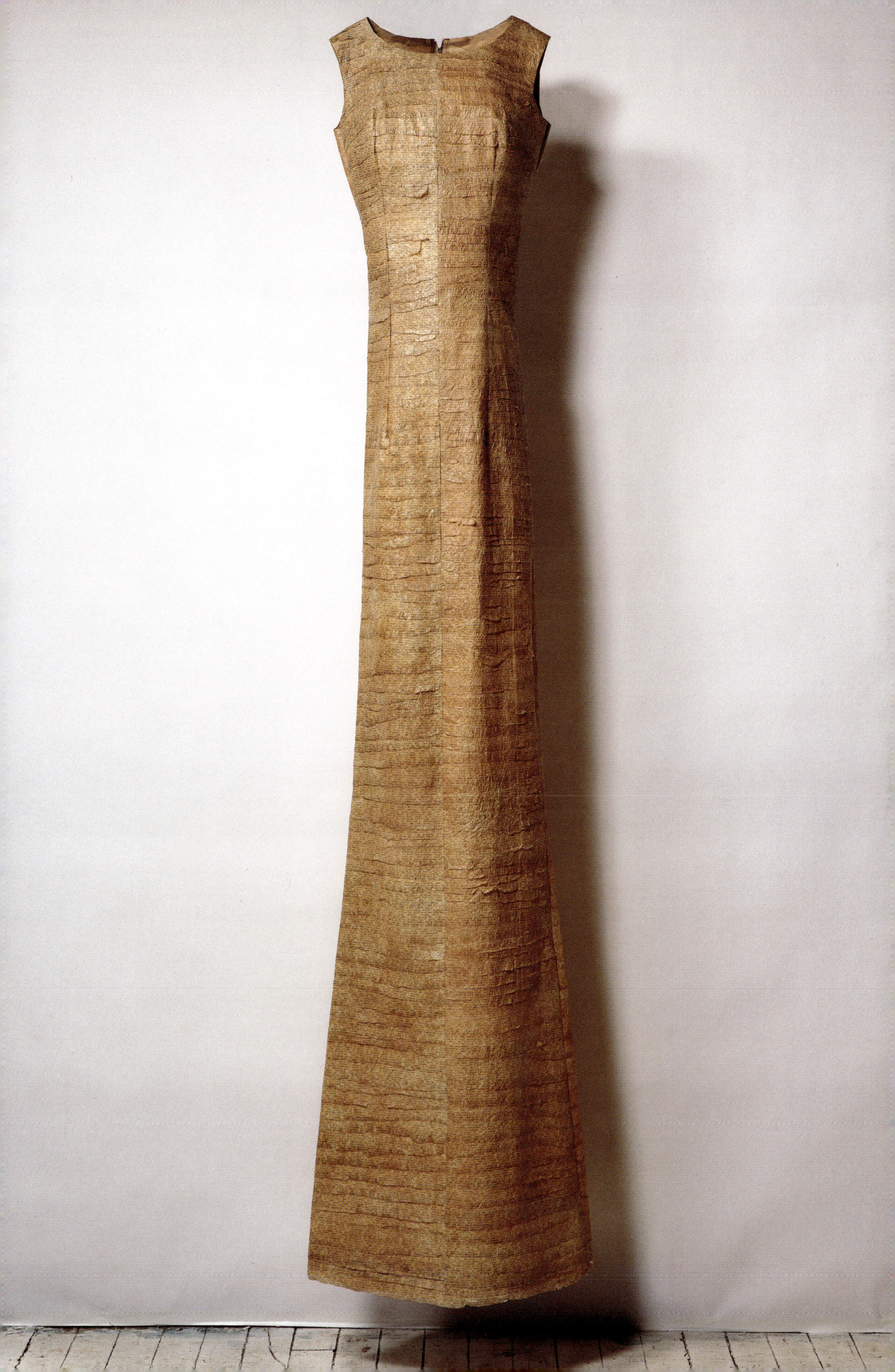

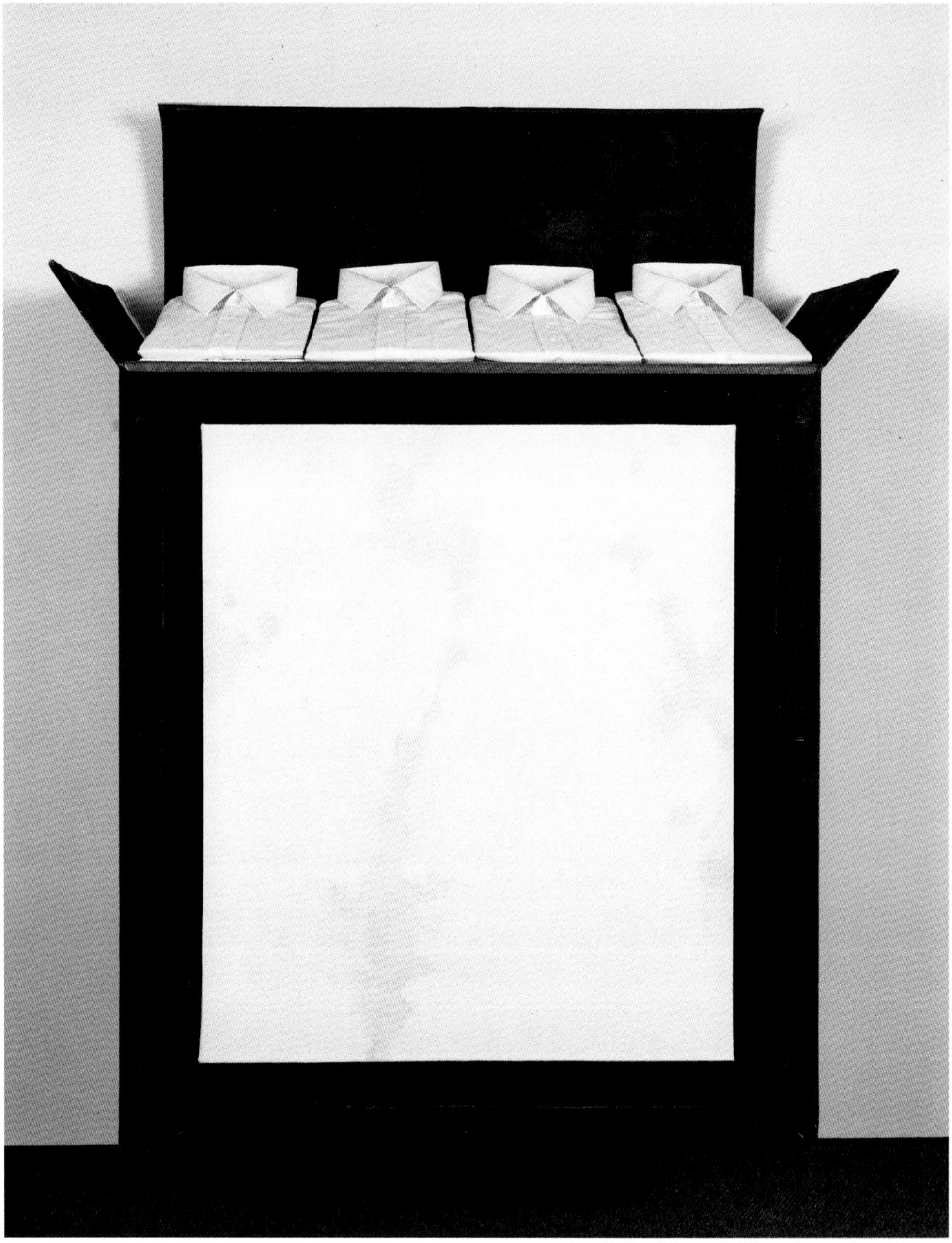

Cameron Shaw, *Untitled Box with White Panel Five Infant Shirts and Twelve Adult Shirts*, 1989, 52 x 41 x 15½"

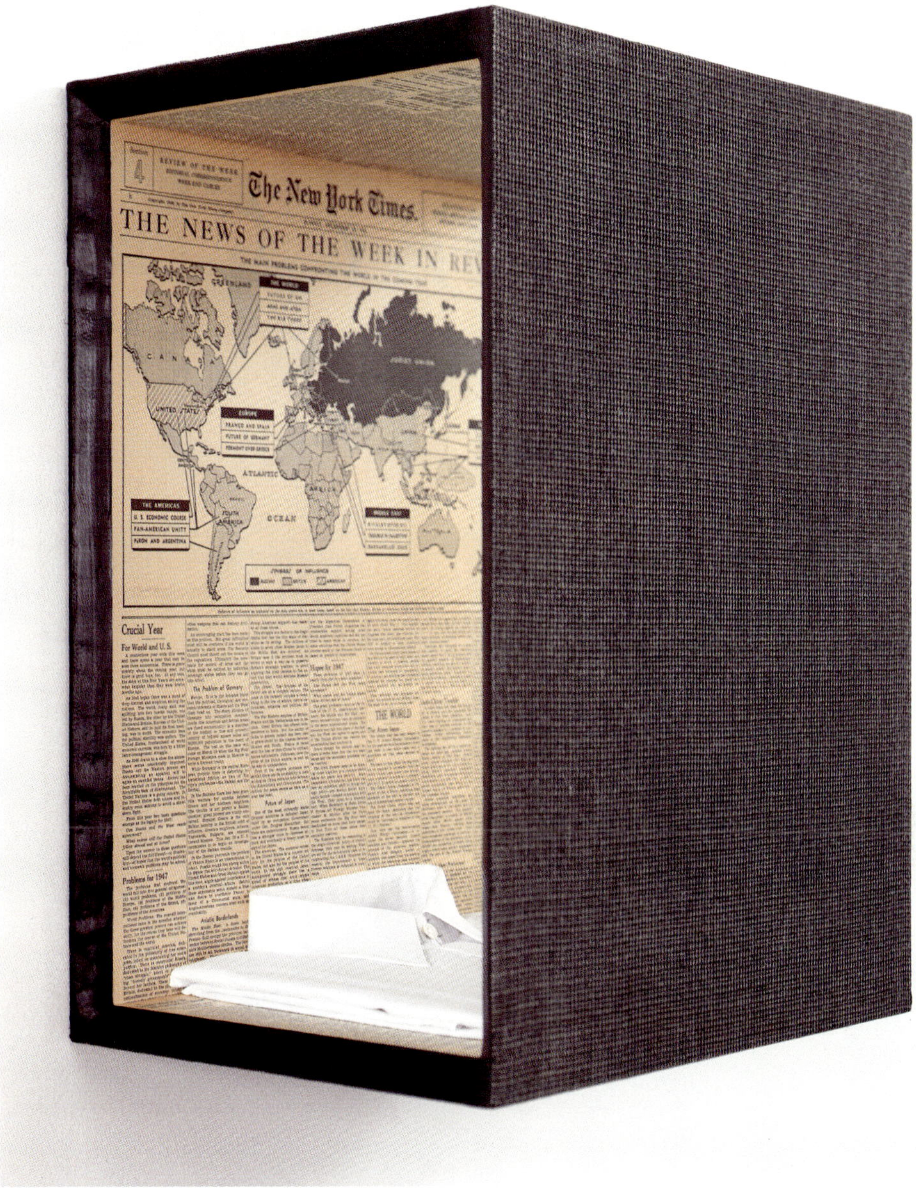

Cameron Shaw, *Refuge #28*, 1992, 23 x 17¼ x 13¾"

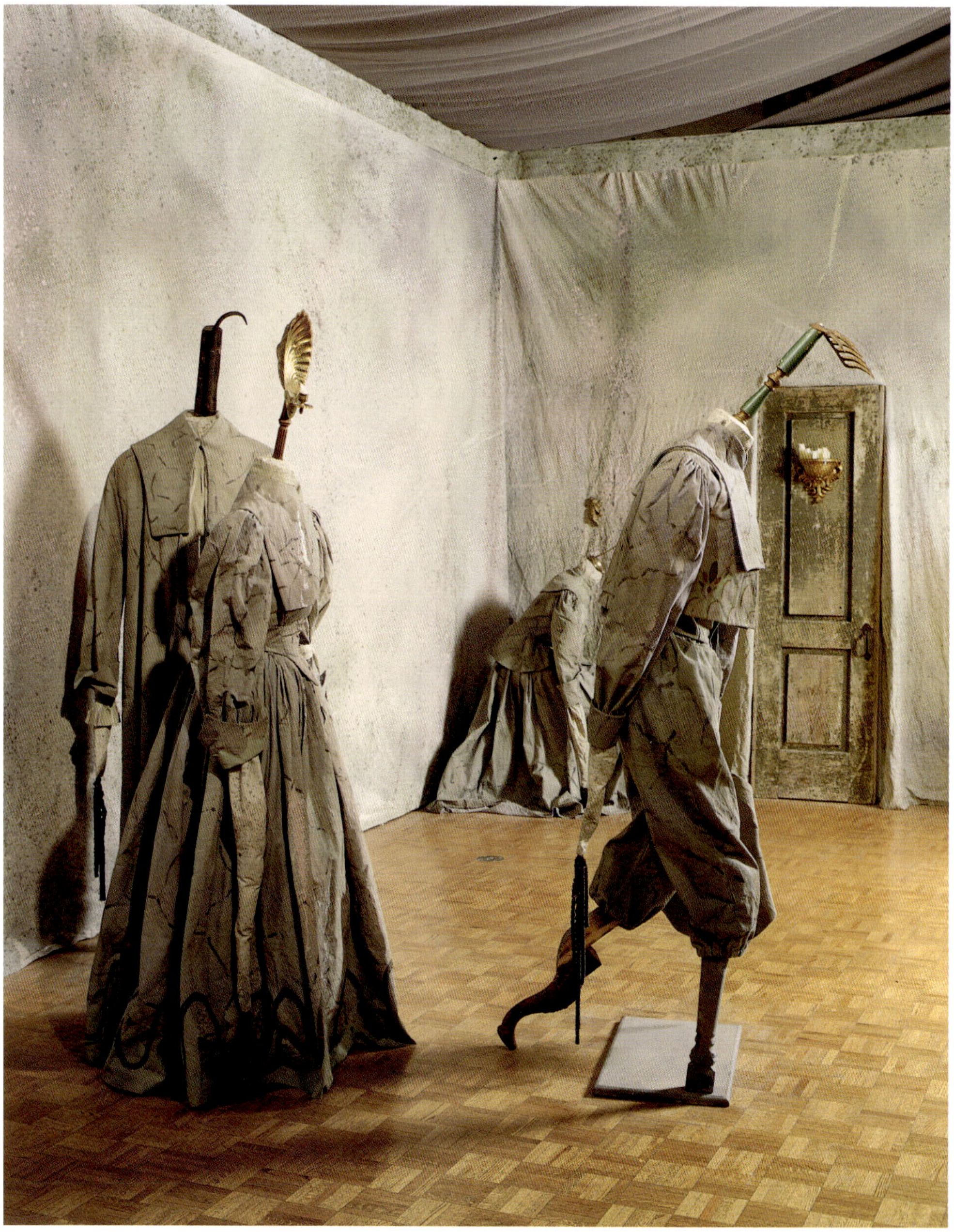

Above: Pamela Keech, *Lust & Etiquette*, detail, 1992-93, 169 x 240 x 204"

Right: *Lust & Etiquette*, detail

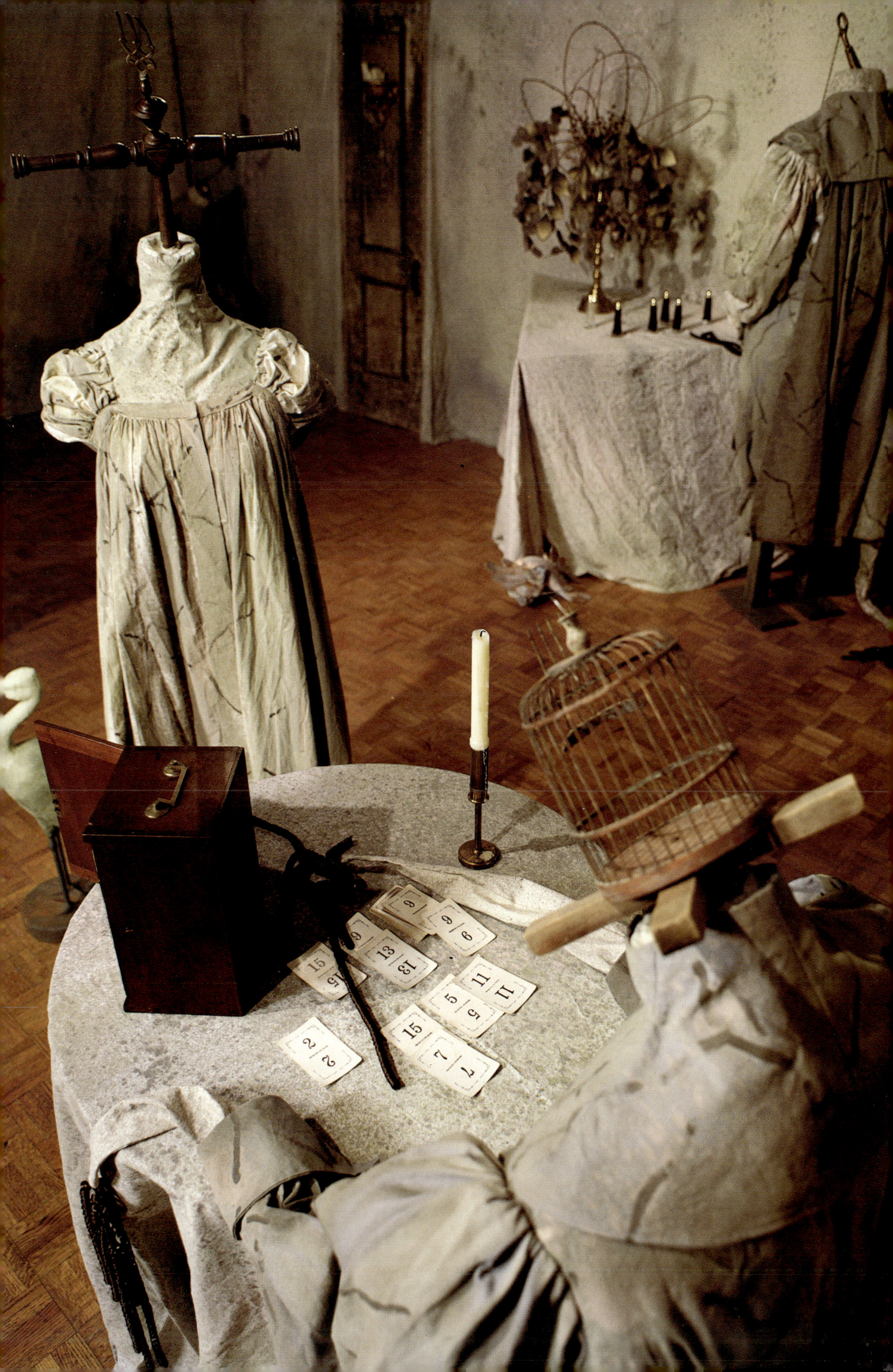
9
6
13
15
11
5
2
15
7

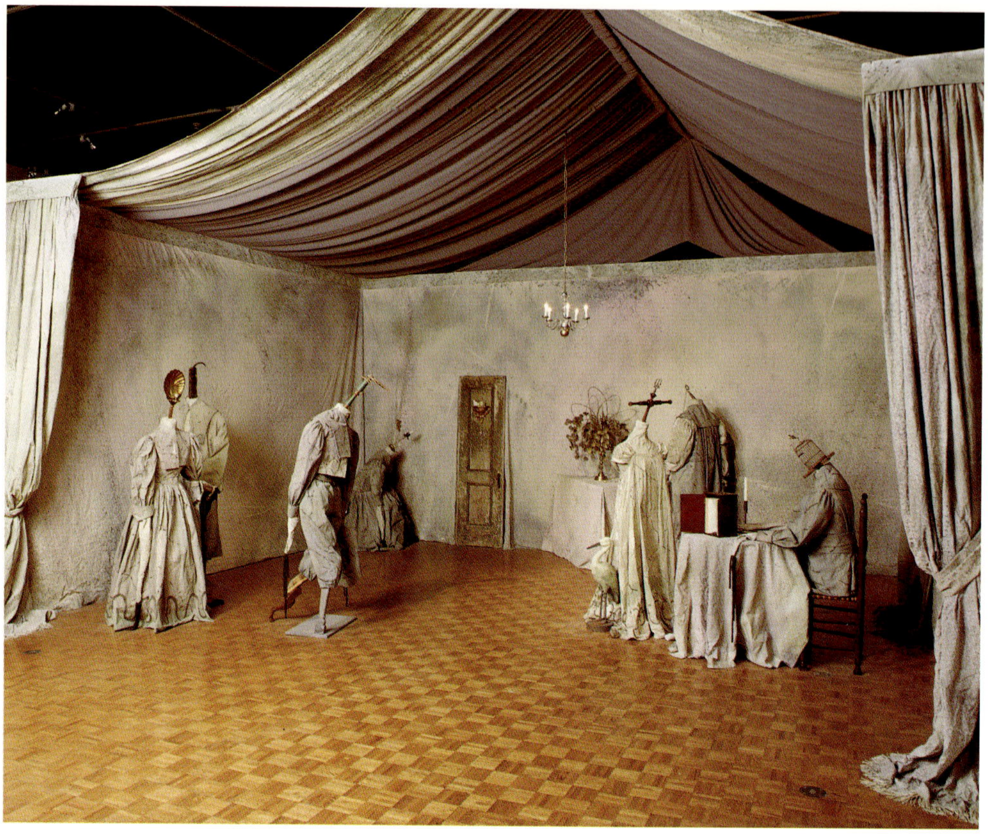

Pamela Keech, *Lust & Etiquette*, 1992-93, 169 x 240 x 204"

Catalogue of Works

MICHELE BLONDEL
New York

1. ***Concue...Baptisee...Communiante***
1987
Steel, opal crystal, and cotton;
69 x 142¼ x 56" (175.3 x 361.3 x 142.2 cm)
Courtesy of Elga Wimmer Gallery, New York
(illustrated page 24)

MAUREEN CONNOR
New York

2. ***Thinner Than You***
1990
Stainless steel and cloth;
60 x 15 x 7½" (152.4 x 38.1 x 19.1 cm)
Courtesy of Germans van Eck Gallery, New York
(illustrated page 26)

3. ***Wishing Well***
1990
Cloth, rubber, and pennies;
138½ x 7" diameter (351.8 x 17.8 cm diameter)
Courtesy of Germans van Eck Gallery, New York

4. ***Untitled***
1990
Steel, body suit, rubber, and mirrors;
132½ x 42¼ x 42¼" (336.6 x 107.3 x 107.3 cm)
Courtesy of Germans van Eck Gallery, New York
(illustrated page 27)

DAVID ECKARD
Oregon

5. ***Hoop Skirt***
1992
Steel, canvas, muslin, and rubber;
61¼ x 42 x 40¾" (155.6 x 106.7 x 103.5 cm)
Loaned by the artist
(illustrated page 17)

6. ***Trousseau***
1991
Canvas, muslin, elastic, wood, sand, and steel;
installation 56 x 186 x 16¾"
(142.2 x 472.4 x 42.5 cm)
Loaned by the artist

JESSE GOODE
New York

7. ***Coats***
1991
Wool, cotton, nylon, polyester, and leather;
164½ x 230½ x 5¼" (417.8 x 585.5 x 13.3 cm)
Loaned by the artist
(illustrated page viii)

PAMELA KEECH
New York

8. ***Lust & Etiquette***
1992-1993
Mixed-media installation;
169 x 240 x 204" (429.3 x 609.6 x 518.2 cm)
Loaned by the artist
(illustrated pages 32, 33, and 34)

ELIZABETH LEISTER
Pennsylvania

9. ***Untitled (Wedding Dress)***
1992
Plastic sheeting, hanger, embroidery;
124 x 58 x 97" (315.0 x 147.3 x 246.4 cm)
Loaned by the artist
(illustrated page vi)

CHRISTINE LoFASO
Rhode Island

10. ***Shift***
1992
Paper, stained with tea; interfacing;
88 x 21 x 11" (223.5 x 53.3 x 27.9 cm)
Loaned by the artist
(illustrated pages 28 and 29)

11. ***Lady's Mantle***
1992
Paper stained with the flower Lady's Mantle;
interfacing; 16½ x 17¼ x 8" (41.9 x 43.8 x 20.3 cm)
Loaned by the artist

CHRISTINE LoFASO (Continued)

12. ***Redress***
    1992
    Gestation Corset
    Paper, stained with catnip; mink fur, buttons, metal eyelets, and lacing; 23½ x 16 x 13" (59.7 x 40.6 x 33.0 cm)
    (illustrated cover and back cover)

    Codpiece
    Paper, stained with the flower Lady's Slipper; fake fur; 7 x 5 x 4" (17.8 x 12.7 x 10.2 cm)
    Loaned by the artist

NAOMI LONDON
Montreal

13. ***The Sweater Project***
    1991 - 1992
    Wool, knitted; gelatin-silver prints, glass and wood frames; 131 x 183 x 5" (332.7 x 464.8 x 12.7 cm)
    Courtesy of the artist, Galerie Lallouz & Watterson, Montreal, and Stux Gallery, New York
    (illustrated pages 20 and 21)

SHARON McCONNELL
Connecticut

14. ***Angel***
    1991
    Hog gut and zipper, hand sewn; washtub and water; 68 x 25¾ x 14" (172.7 x 65.4 x 35.6 cm)
    Loaned by the artist
    (illustrated pages 22 and 23)

15. ***Fugitive***
    1992 - 1993
    Hog gut, egg yolk, and egg dust; 108 x 78 x 4¼" (274.3 x 198.1 x 10.8 cm)
    Loaned by the artist
    (illustrated page 22)

YONG SOON MIN
California

16. ***Remembering Chungshindae***
    1992
    Korean dress, hand and machine stitched; modeling paste, soil, wax, charcoal, pine needles, and red light; 62½ x 55 x 31" (158.8 x 139.7 x 78.7 cm)
    Loaned by the artist
    (illustrated pages 18 and 19)

CAMERON SHAW
Massachusetts

17. ***Untitled Box with White Panel Five Infant Shirts and Twelve Adult Shirts***
    1989
    Beeswax, wool, wood, cotton, and shirts; 52 x 41 x 15½" (132.1 x 104.1 x 39.4 cm)
    From the collection of Alan Dinsfriend, Massachusetts
    (illustrated page 30)

18. ***Refuge #28***
    1992
    Beeswax, wool, wood, newsprint, and shirt; 23 x 17¼ x 13¾" (58.4 x 43.8 x 34.9 cm)
    Courtesy of the artist and Barbara Krakow Gallery, Massachusetts
    (illustrated page 31)

19. ***Untitled Open Box with Washington's Letter and Three Shirts***
    1990
    Beeswax, wool, wood, shirts, photograph, and lead; 30½ x 38½ x 16¾" (77.5 x 97.8 x 42.5 cm)
    From the collection of R. Anne McCarthy, Massachusetts

20. ***Untitled Stack with Katzenjammer Kids and Blue Shirt***
    1992
    Beeswax, wool, wood, newsprint, cotton, and cast iron; 54½ x 18½ x 18½" (138.4 x 47.0 x 47.0 cm)
    Loaned by the artist

ALLAN WEXLER
New York

21. ***Four White Shirts Sewn into a Tablecloth***
    1991
    Linen tablecloth and cotton shirts, machine stitched; 128 x 120 x 2" (325.1 x 304.8 x 5.1 cm)
    Courtesy of Ronald Feldman Fine Arts, Inc., New York

22. ***Four Shirt Collars Sewn into a Tablecloth***
    1991
    Linen tablecloth and cotton shirt collars, machine stitched; 71 x 62 x 2" (180.3 x 157.5 x 5.1 cm)
    Courtesy of Ronald Feldman Fine Arts, Inc., New York
    (illustrated page 25)

Select Bibliography

Ash, Juliet and Elizabeth Wilson. *Chic Thrills: A Fashion Reader.* Berkeley: University of California Press, 1993.

Barthes, Roland. *The Responsibility of Forms.* New York: Farrar, Strauss and Giroux, 1985.

Bolton, Richard. "Beauty Redefined: From Ideal Form to Experiential Meaning." *New Art Examiner* (November 1993): 27-31.

Gaines, Jane. "Introduction: Fabricating the Female Body." *Fabrications: Costume and the Female Body*, edited by Jane Gaines and Charlotte Herzog, 1-27. New York and London: Routledge, 1990.

Hall, Donald, Thomas Laqueur, and Helaine Posner. *Corporal Politics.* Cambridge and Boston: MIT List Visual Arts Center and Beacon Press, 1992.

Kaplan, Cora. "The Thorn Birds: Fiction, Fantasy, Femininity." *Formations of Fantasy*, edited by Victor Burgin, James Donald, and Cora Kaplan, 142-166. London: Methuen and Co. Ltd., 1986.

Kunzle, David. *Fashion and Fetishism: A Social History of the Corset, Tight-Lacing and Other Forms of Body-Sculpture in the West.* Totowa, New Jersey: Rowman and Littlefield, 1982.

Martin, Richard. "Approximating the Body." *New Art Examiner* (September 1993): 16-18.

Perniola, Mario. "Between Clothing and Nudity." *Zone: Fragments for a History of the Human Body*, Part Two, edited by Michel Feher with Ramona Naddaff and Nadia Tazi, 236-265. New York: Urzone, Inc., 1989.

Silverman, Kaja. "Fragments of a Fashionable Discourse." *Studies in Entertainment: Critical Approaches to Mass Culture*, edited by Tania Modleski, 139-152. Bloomington and Indianapolis: Indiana University Press, 1986.

Wilson, Elizabeth. *Adorned in Dreams: Fashion and Modernity.* London: Virago, 1985.

Wollen, Peter. "Fashion/Orientalism/The Body." *New Formations* (Volume 1, Spring 1987): 5-33.

JOHN MICHAEL KOHLER ARTS CENTER STAFF

Ruth DeYoung Kohler, director

EXHIBITIONS

Alison Ferris, curator of exhibitions
Emil Donoval, registrar
James Mazur, preparator/technical coordinator
Laureen O'Toole Kelly, curatorial assistant

PERFORMING ARTS

Aviva Davidson, performing arts coordinator
Darlene Geiger, performing arts assistant
Eric R. Johnson, photographer/performing arts technical coordinator

ARTS/INDUSTRY

Lynne Shumow, Arts/Industry coordinator
Peter Flanary, Arts/Industry technician
Paul Sebben, Arts/Industry technician

EDUCATION

Brian Reindl, education coordinator
Gina Kallman, education assistant
Judy Conger, Preschool administrator/instructor
Cathy Perronne, assistant Preschool instructor

ARTSPACE/FLYING COLORS

Jean Lorrigan Puls, artistic coordinator -Artspace/Flying Colors
Linda Van Sistine-Yost, administrative coordinator - Flying Colors/Artspace
Ingrid Wenniger, bookkeeper - Artspace/Flying Colors
Nola Maury, Artspace associate
Michele Mikulay, Artspace associate

DEVELOPMENT

Mary Jo McBrearty, manager - community development
Ellen Clark, special events/grants coordinator

MARKETING/PRESENTATION

Patti Glaser-Martin, publicity administrator
Karl Janssen, designer of publications

ADMINISTRATION

Rebecca Perry Damsen, assistant director for administration
Sally Bohenstengel, accountant
Dave Kudek, human resources coordinator
Dorothy Hellauer, word processing specialist
Jane Andrews, secretary/receptionist I
Deborah Sandven, accounting assistant
Ron Krepsky, technician
Nancy Dummer, administrative assistant
Jill Stegner, office assistant
Allison Lance, secretary/receptionist II
Kate Wegman, secretary/receptionist II

ARTISTS ADVISORY BOARD

Mark Anderson
Joe Bruchac
Carole Byard
Yreina Cervantez
Patrick Dougherty
Katharine Kreisher
Ken Little
Tom Uttech
Anne Wilson
Jawole Willa Jo Zollar

COLOPHON

Separations by Rayson Films, Inc., Waukesha, Wisconsin
Plates by Wisconsin Graphic Plate, Inc., Sheboygan, Wisconsin
Printed by Universal Lithographers, Inc., Sheboygan, Wisconsin
Paper Stock: Warren Patina 100# text and cover
Typestyle: Goudy
Photo Credits:
Thaddeus Govan: pages 26 and 27
Peter Hernandez of Irish Photography Studio: page vi
Eric R. Johnson: pages viii, 17, 18, 19, 20, 21, 22, 23, 25, 32, 33, 34
Gerry Kobylecky: front and back covers and pages 28 and 29
John Lamkon (photo courtesy of Elga Wimmer Gallery): page 24
Cameron Shaw: pages 30 and 31
Kati Toivanen: page 22